The Barbados-Carolina Connection

Warren Alleyne and Henry Fraser

MACMILLAN
CARIBBEAN

First published 1988

Published by *Macmillan Publishers Ltd*
London and Basingstoke
Associated companies and representatives in Accra,
Auckland, Delhi, Dublin, Gaborone, Hamburg, Harare,
Hong Kong, Kuala Lumpur, Lagos, Manzini, Melbourne,
Mexico City, Nairobi, New York, Singapore, Tokyo

Printed in Hong Kong

British Library Cataloguing in Publication Data
Alleyne, Warren, *1924–*
    The Barbados—Caroloina connection.
    1. Barbados. Relations, 1660–1987 with
    Carolina   2. Carolina. Relations, 1660–
    1987 with Barbados
    I. Title   II. Fraser, Henry
    303.4′8272981′0756

ISBN 0–333–47345–0

Acknowledgements

The authors and publishers wish to express their thanks to
those who have kindly provided photographs for this book.

Cover illustrations

Front
Middleton Place, Charleston (*photograph by Henry Fraser*)
St Nicholas Abbey, Barbados (*photograph by Henry Fraser*)
Back
Warren Alleyne by the Stede Bonnet Monument in Charleston
(*photograph by Henry Fraser*)
Henry Fraser in front of Old Mill Wall, near his residence
at Upton (formerly Bonnets Plantation and the property of
the pirate Stede Bonnet) (*photograph by Bill Grace*)

Contents

Authors' Preface

Few Barbadians or Americans have been aware of the close connection that exists between Barbados and the Carolinas—of the exploration of the Carolina coast by the Barbados Adventurers, of the part played in the settlement of Charles Town in 1670 and the intimate links of the next hundred years. Indeed many modern books on Charleston have ignored the connection. But the South Carolina Tricentennial in 1970, and the writings of historians like Professor George Rogers of the University of South Carolina, Dr Joseph Waring of Charleston and American resident of Barbados, May Lumsden, have put the relationship into a better perspective, both to academic historians and to the lay public of Barbados and Charleston.

Increasing interest in the subject by the Barbados Board of Tourism culminated in an invitation to the authors to visit Charleston in 1985 to do research on the historical links and the possible architectural links. A great deal has been written on the early settlement and on genealogies of Charlestonians from Barbados, but the facts about some of the earliest migrants remained shrouded in mystery. And in spite of the strong tradition that the Charleston Single House came from Barbados, there has been no known research on this subject. Finally, few people are aware of the uncanny similarities in accent and content between our Bajan dialect and the Gullah dialect of old Charlestonians. So it was with great excitement that our team, led by Manager of the Board in New York, Markly Wilson, set off for Charleston. This book is the fruit of that visit and a great deal of further research.

We greatly appreciate the opportunity afforded us by the Barbados Board of Tourism of carrying out this project, and we are indebted to the inspiration, personal involvement and superb organisation of Mr Markly Wilson (Manager, USA) who co-ordinated the research visit and created many contacts. He even discovered a hotel, the Mills

Map of Barbados from *A True and Exact History of Barbados*, Richard Ligon, 1657

Hyatt House with its superb dining room the 'Barbadoes Room', so that we could savour even the culinary connections!

We must thank the former Chairman of the Board, Mr Jack Dear, the Director of Tourism, Mrs Pat Nehaul; former Public Relations Manager, Mrs Margaret Hope and Public Relations Officer, Ms Cheryl Carter; Lady Chandler, who shared her personal collection of Charleston-Barbados documents with us; Mr Henry Cauthen of the Charleston Preservation Society, Mr Gary Brandershute, Mr Drayton Hastie, Ms Virginia Gerahty, Professor George Rogers, Mr Ken Severens, Dr George Terry and many other Carolinians or Charlestonians who hosted us, guided us or advised us about Charleston. And we are most grateful to Mr Bill Lennox, Director of Macmillan Caribbean, for developing with us the idea of a book which would bring this exciting story to popular attention, and for waiting patiently for us to marshal our facts, our ideas and our pictures.

Finally, we are grateful to all those who lent us materials or answered questions, to Ronnie Hughes for helpful comments, and to Enid Carter, Marcia Murrell and Grace Ifill for their intuitive mastery of our manuscript.

Drayton Hall, Charleston, South Carolina (*Felix Kerr*)

1 Barbados— Gateway to America

The island of Barbados is the most easterly of the West Indian islands. It lies in the Atlantic, 13°04′ North and 59°37′ West, 100 miles east of the chain of islands known as the Lesser Antilles, and is technically outside the Caribbean Sea. In shape it resembles a leg of lamb, and it is approximately 166 square miles, or 430 square kilometres, in area.

Mainly of coral formation, Barbados is not mountainous, like most of the neighbouring islands, and most of the land can be cultivated. It rises in terraces from Bridgetown in the southwest to a plateau of about 1,000 feet in the northeast; from there it descends steeply to the rugged east coast. The highest point is only 1,116 feet.

Although Barbados was never visited by Christopher Columbus, its existence must have been known to the Spaniards by 1500, and to the Portuguese soon afterwards, for the island of Los Barbados is mentioned in Spanish cedulas – formal official orders – of 23 December 1511 and 3 July 1512; on each occasion it came first in a list of islands.

The origin of the name, which means 'The Bearded Ones' in Portuguese, is uncertain. According to one theory, the island owes its name to the presence of Indians with beards who were living there when it was discovered. The more popular theory attributes the name to the large number of a species of fig tree (*Ficus citrifolia*) which sends down clusters of many aerial roots suggestive of beards. A Bearded Fig Tree 'eradicated' (uprooted) is the principal device on the Barbados Coat of Arms, and it features in a stylized form on the island's Royal flag, or Sovereign's Standard for Barbados.

Pedro a Campos, a Portuguese mariner sailing to Brazil, landed at Barbados in 1536. He found the island uninhabited and he is credited with having thoughtfully left a number of hogs to multiply as a source of food for any seamen who might be shipwrecked.

The first Englishman who claims to have landed on Barbados was a

The bearded fig tree (*ficus citrifolia*) in the famous Andromeda Gardens at Bathsheba, St Joseph, Barbados (*Tony Seddon*)

Captain Simon Gordon in 1620 and, like Pedro a Campos, he found no inhabitants. Archaeological evidence confirms the historical evidence that Barbados was inhabited by Amerindians as late as the beginning of the sixteenth century.

The First Settlement

In 1625 the *Olive*, an English ship homeward bound from Brazil, called at Barbados (some accounts call her the *Olive Blossom*). Her captain, John Powell, decided to explore the island, and after sailing along the south and west coasts, he landed at what is now Holetown as well as at a site near present-day Bridgetown. At both places he performed symbolic ceremonies claiming Barbados for the English Crown.

John Powell's employers were the brothers (and merchants) Sir William and Sir Peter Courteen. When he reported all this to them and explained the potential of the island for development, they decided to establish a settlement. The ship *William and John*, under the command of John Powell's brother, Henry Powell, landed in Barbados, again at Holetown, in February 1627, bringing ten African slaves who had somehow been acquired during the voyage.

The settlers erected some wooden houses for shelter. Although there were wild hogs for hunting, thanks perhaps to Pedro a Campos, the island offered no food-producing plants other than a few fruit trees. Fortunately, Henry Powell was a friend of the Governor of the Dutch settlement of Guiana and, through his good offices, Powell was able to obtain not only a variety of plants and seeds, but also some Amerindians to instruct the settlers in their cultivation.

The next two and a half years were an unhappy period because of conflicting claims to land. As John Powell had taken possession of Barbados on behalf of the Crown, the settlers could have no rights except those granted by the Crown, and authority to English subjects to establish colonies overseas normally took the form of Letters Patent, or Charters, issued by the Crown.

In July 1627, less than five months after the arrival of the Courteen expedition in Barbados, Charles I by Patent made James Hay, Earl of Carlisle, Lord Proprietor of Barbados and of certain other islands in the area. Carlisle was then heavily in debt to a syndicate of London merchants, and he immediately granted 10,000 acres of Barbadian land to these merchants to liquidate his debts. They appointed Charles Wolferstone of Bermuda their administrator.

However, in February 1628, before the Merchants' expedition sailed, and while Carlisle was absent from England, Charles I issued a Patent in almost identical terms to the Earl of Pembroke and Montgomery, whom the Courteens had asked to act on their behalf. But when Carlisle remonstrated, naturally, on his return from abroad, the King issued him a new Patent as Lord Proprietor—a recipe for total confusion!

Wolferstone arrived at Barbados as the Merchants' Governor in June 1628 with 64 settlers, and established a new settlement around Carlisle Bay. Fully aware that the Courteen settlers to Leeward (to the north) were unwilling to abandon their claims, he at first avoided taking any provocative action, but finally the parties came close to conflict. They met at Palmetto Fort at Holetown but a clergyman apparently procured a truce. Wolferstone managed to establish his authority, and placed their leader, John Powell, in confinement.

In February the next year, 1629, when Henry Powell arrived at Barbados with a fresh batch of Courteen settlers, Wolferstone was kidnapped and carried off to England, and John Powell was reinstated!

Captain Henry Hawley then arrived on the Earl of Carlisle's behalf and treacherously kidnapped John Powell in his turn, leaving one of the Carlisle merchants as Governor. It became clear, however, that Courteen had lost the struggle, and all further efforts made by him and his heirs failed to produce compensation for his great financial losses.

In December that same year, 1629, Sir William Tufton arrived as Governor for the Earl of Carlisle. Although the population was still too small to warrant all the paraphernalia of government, Tufton set about the task of establishing law and order. His most notable achievement, perhaps, was the division of the island into six parishes, each with a parish church and minister and an elected vestry or parish council on the English pattern. He also tried to ameliorate the cruel treatment by masters of their Christian servants, which may have made him unpopular with some of the planters.

Whether it was a result of this, or whether it was pure craftiness on the part of Captain Hawley, a most unprincipled man, in 1630 Hawley arrived with a commission from Carlisle to replace Tufton. His arbitrary rule soon provoked Tufton into organising a petition against him, with the result that Tufton was arbitrarily tried for mutiny and executed.

Hawley governed Barbados from 1630 until he was removed by his employers under threat of force ten years later. His connection with the island had begun with the expedition of 1629 and it ended ignominiously with his death in 1677—reputedly from injuries sustained when he fell downstairs in a tavern he owned in Bridgetown!

Henry Hawley is best remembered as the person who introduced representative government in Barbados. But even so, his motives (and his methods) were questionable. In 1639 he realised that he was about to be removed from office by the new Proprietor, the Second Earl of Carlisle. As a last ditch attempt to enlist local support he summoned an elected Assembly for inclusion into the Legislature. More than likely, the two representatives drawn from each parish had been handpicked by him. In fact, an Assemblyman, Captain Fuller, asked 'if all whoremasters were taken off the Bench, what would the Governor do for a Council?' Hawley responded by putting him in the pillory at high noon without a hat!

The man appointed in 1640 to replace Hawley was Henry Huncks, a soldier, believed to be of Dutch extraction. He soon proved a poor administrator, and was recalled the next year.

Philip Bell, his successor, was by contrast an able man who, during his nine-year administration, did much to improve the island's judicial system. The House of Assembly, hitherto a purely advisory body, acquired the right to initiate legislation, and altogether the colony began to advance economically and socially.

Sugar and Slavery

The first crops grown in Barbados for export were tobacco and cotton. Tobacco soon proved unprofitable because it was clearly inferior to that grown in Virginia, and it was abandoned when the planters discovered that about three times the value of sugar could be grown on the same acreage.

Sugar production started about 1640. The initial capital outlay was heavy, as the buildings, called sugar works, were costly. But sugar offered prospects of wealth, and planters who could afford it expanded their holdings to several hundred acres. By 1650 sugar had become firmly established as the island's dominant crop, and has remained so

Old sugar mill at Drax Hall, Barbados, where the growing of sugar cane began around 1640 (*Felix Kerr*)

ever since. By the 1650s it was producing intoxicating wealth and Barbados was 'the richest colony in English America.'

As a large labour force was needed to sustain the sugar industry, slaves were imported from Africa in great numbers. Soon they largely replaced the indentured servants and outnumbered the whites who, nevertheless, exercised all political and economic power for nearly another three centuries.

The introduction of sugar also caused large scale migration from Barbados. The small farmers who had arrived in the thirties were unable to compete with the large plantations, and were gradually squeezed out. 8,300 landholders are reckoned to have been in the island in 1643. By 1666 much of the land held by them had been amalgamated into larger properties with 760 considerable proprietors.

A *Report on Barbados* published in 1667 mentioned that some 12,000 good men, formerly proprietors, had gone off the island together with tradesmen who had been 'wormed' out of their small settlements by greedy neighbours! (The number was probably an overestimate.) Their destinations were such places as New England, Virginia, Surinam and other Caribbean islands, particularly Jamaica.

It was this drive for new lands which stimulated the exploration of Carolina by Barbadians and the subsequent settlement of Charleston; Barbados in the 1660s was to become the gateway to America, or at least to the Carolinas, Jamaica, Guiana and much of the Caribbean.

2
The Adventurers

The Barbadians were not the first to attempt settlement of the territory that was later named Carolina. The first Europeans were the Spaniards, who made several efforts between 1521 and 1562 to establish themselves at Port Royal, not very far north of what is now the border of the State of Georgia.

Then in 1562 a group of Huguenots – French Protestants – started a settlement at the same place, but they abandoned this within two years. The Spaniards returned in 1566, only to be driven out by the Indians. In 1587 they finally gave up the idea of settling the territory, and no further efforts were made to colonise the region for nearly a century.

This was an era when the Sovereigns of Europe – more particularly those of England and France – freely bestowed charters and territorial grants on individuals or companies. As has been mentioned, the two Patents of Charles I of England caused trouble. In October 1629 he granted to his Attorney-General, Sir Robert Heath, 'all that territory in America lying between 31 and 36 degrees north latitude'. This territory would today extend from the Atlantic to the Pacific. It was given the name Carolana in the king's honour—*Carolana*, not *Carolina* at this stage.

But this huge grant was never exploited, either by Sir Robert Heath or by his heirs. It was not until the third year after the restoration of Charles II that eight aristocrats who had supported him throughout his long exile during the Cromwellian regime in Britain, and had helped him back to his throne, obtained a charter for the same territory, now to be renamed Carolina. This charter, dated 24 March 1663, was similar in many respects to that of 1629. It embodied many of its provisions, permitting nothing less than feudal power in the government of the territory.

It was this charter which saw the start of the 'Barbados-Carolina Connection'. Sir John Colleton, a prominent Barbadian planter, had suggested to Anthony Ashley Cooper (Baron Ashley of Wimborne St Giles, later first Earl of Shaftesbury) that in association with certain others they should 'petition the king for a grant of this rich and fertile Province'. Colleton, incidentally, was one of thirteen Barbadian loyalists who were created knights or baronets in the years after the Restoration of Charles II. Lord Ashley had previously owned a plantation in Barbados in the parish of St George.

The Lords Proprietors of Carolina

The eight noblemen to whom the charter was granted were Edward Hyde, Earl of Clarendon; George Monck, Duke of Albemarle; William, Lord Craven; John, Lord Berkeley; Lord Ashley; Sir George Carteret; Sir William Berkeley and, of course, Sir John Colleton, recently created baronet. This group became known as the Lords Proprietors of Carolina.

Another Barbadian who was soon to become closely involved in the settlement was Sir John Yeamans, whose baronetcy was conferred in January 1665 on the recommendation of the Lords Proprietors.

News of the Carolina grant of 1663 was greatly welcomed by many planters in Barbados, where land had become scarce and expensive. A number of them at once formed a syndicate called the Corporation of Barbados Adventurers, and their leaders, Thomas Modyford, a former Governor of Barbados, and Peter Colleton, a son of Sir John, began preparing proposals for submission to the Lords Proprietors for the settlement of a colony.

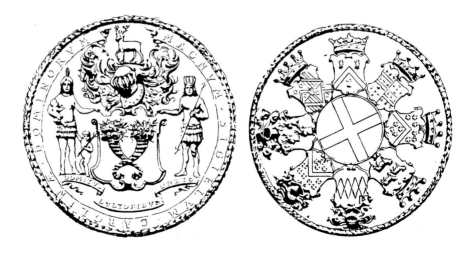

The seal of the Lords Proprietors

On 12 August 1663, Modyford and Colleton at last addressed a petition to the Proprietors proposing that the Adventurers, who numbered about 200 including many 'persons of good quality', might be permitted to purchase from the Indians a tract of 1,000 miles in Carolina, and asked that they might be granted certain powers of self-government.

The First Expedition

Without waiting for a response from the Lords Proprietors, the Adventurers sent out an exploratory expedition in a ship appropriately named the *Adventure*, commanded by Captain William Hilton. Hilton had previously made a voyage to the coast of what is now North Carolina; and he had made favourable reports about the country near the Cape Fear river. He was now sent to explore the coast southward from that region to latitude 31° North. The *Adventure*, with a crew of 22, and provisions for seven months, sailed from the bay at Speightstown on 10 August 1663 and, reaching the Carolina coast on the following 26 August, began the search for a suitable place for settlement.

Captain Hilton began the return voyage to Barbados on 4 December, and on 6 January 1664 he anchored in Carlisle Bay. His account of his explorations was published in London later that year. Hilton's memory has been preserved in the names of both Hilton Head and Hilton Island, a promontory and an island on the coast of North Carolina.

But the Lords Proprietors did not accept the proposals for self-government submitted by the Barbados Adventurers and nothing came of this first attempt to settle Carolina.

Meanwhile, another group of Barbadians headed by John Vassall and Richard Evans had obtained concessions to establish a settlement in the Province. Their success may be due to the fact that this second group included a substantial number of wealthy men. But perhaps what weighed heavily in their favour was that a good many of them had served in the Barbados legislature or in local government, and were thus qualified to run a colony. In 1664 they established a colony called Charles Towne near the Cape Fear River.

Sir John Yeamans Takes Charge

However, the Proprietors were now anxious to encourage settlement of their grant and in January 1665 they signed an agreement with another group of Barbadian Adventurers, numbering some 85. This group was headed by Sir John Yeamans and included a substantial number of wealthy and influential men. Under the terms of this agreement each Adventurer was to receive 500 acres of land for every 1,000 pounds weight of sugar he contributed. A further grant of 150 acres was to be made to every person who would sail with Yeamans on the first fleet to Carolina.

Yeamans himself received a grant of 6,000 acres from the Lords Proprietors, who at the same time appointed him 'Governor of their County of Clarendon near Cape Fear and all that tract southerly as far as the river St Matthias, and west as far as the South Seas, with power to appoint twelve able men at most, and six at least, to be of his Council unless the Lords Proprietors have before made choice of all or any of them.' In addition, Yeamans was appointed Lieutenant-General of all Forces to be raised in the County.

Sir John Yeamans sailed from Barbados for Cape Fear in October 1665, to take up his appointment. His own frigate was accompanied by a sloop and a flyboat, but while trying to navigate the Cape Fear river the flyboat, with most of the provisions and twelve pieces of artillery on board, ran aground and was wrecked. This disaster forced Yeamans to alter his plans. He had intended using the sloop to explore, but he found the settlers at Cape Fear in such need that he had to send this vessel to Virginia for supplies. He then returned to Barbados after commissioning the Secretary of the Province, Robert Sandford, to explore the coast as soon as the sloop returned.

Sandford made his exploration in the middle of 1666, and published a glowing account of the territory he had seen.

At Port Royal, one of the places he visited, he had met an Indian Cassique (or chief) of Kiawah, a region some distance further north, who urged him to go there and see what excellent facilities it offered for trade. With the Indian as pilot, Sandford finally arrived at the river leading into the Kiawah country. Although he did not make a landing, he was persuaded that it was indeed an excellent country and he named the river the Ashley in compliment to Lord Ashley.

During 1666, mainly because of the Second Dutch War (1665–67) then in progresss, no more settlers or supplies arrived at Cape Fear from Barbados. The Barbadian colony there consequently became convinced they had been abandoned, and about October 1667 they broke up the settlement and dispersed to the other established colonies of Virginia and New England.

3
The Odyssey

The Lords Proprietors meanwhile had been taking measures to devise a form of government for their proposed province. Directed by Lord Ashley, the renowned philosopher John Locke drew up the famous 'Fundamental Constitutions' for the government of Carolina, which were formally adopted by the Proprietors in July 1669. In their 111 Articles, the Constitutions envisaged an extraordinary scheme for creating an aristocratic (and feudal) government in a land that was still a primitive wilderness.

The charter that had been granted to the Lords Proprietors declared the province a 'County Palatine', and the Fundamental Constitutions provided that the eldest of the Proprietors should be the Palatine or Governor, having the privileges of vice-royalty. They provided also for a feudal society headed by a hereditary nobility comprising two orders of nobility, namely Landgraves and Cassiques, besides the Lords Proprietors themselves.

Each county was to contain 480,000 acres. The eight Proprietors were each to have 96,000 acres. There were to be as many Landgraves as counties and twice as many Cassiques. Each Landgrave was to have 48,000 acres and each Cassique 24,000 acres. The remaining 288,000 acres, or three-fifths of each county were for 'the people'.

Government of the Province was to be through a Grand Council composed of the Proprietors and leading members of the nobility, and an Assembly or Parliament consisting of this same group in combination with lesser nobles and delegates elected by the commoners.

Remarkably for that period, the Fundamental Constitutions guaranteed complete religious freedom. Equally remarkable in that era when, in Barbados for example, the religious instruction of slaves was either prohibited or discouraged, the Constitutions decreed, 'It shall be lawful for slaves, as all others, to enter themselves and be of what church any of them shall think best and thereof be as fully members as any freemen'.

By 1698, some five versions of the Fundamental Constitutions would be drawn up and promulgated. None, however, would be ratified, and a simplified system would be substituted. They would, nonetheless, have an influence on both the political and the social institutions of Carolina.

The Lords Proprietors then turned their attention to colonization. As the first settlement of Barbadians at Cape Fear had failed, they were not interested in re-establishing any new settlement there. They had, however, been impressed with the glowing account Sandford had published in 1666 of the country at Port Royal much farther south, and they decided to send a group of settlers from England, via Barbados, to establish a colony there.

On 26 July 1669, they issued a Commission for the Governor of the Province of Carolina, leaving a space blank for the insertion of the name of Sir John Yeamans or his designate. On the following day they commissioned Joseph West Commander-in-Chief of a fleet of three vessels to transport the first settlers.

The instructions issued to West required him to 'sail with all possible speed' to Kinsale in Ireland, where he was to try to recruit 20 or 25 servants, and then to Barbados before continuing on to Port Royal. On his arrival at Barbados he was to apply to Thomas Colleton, a son of the Proprietor, Sir John Colleton, to furnish him with cotton and indigo seed, ginger roots, canes and other plants for cultivation at the settlement, and to acquire also a boar and six young sows for breeding.

Disaster Strikes

The expedition's three vessels, the *Carolina*, *Port Royal*, and *Albemarle* arrived safely at Barbados around the end of October; but on 2 November the *Albemarle* was driven ashore by a storm and wrecked—the first of a series of misfortunes that were to dog the expedition. A similar vessel, the *Three Brothers*, was bought to replace her, and on 23 November the reconstituted fleet, now joined by Sir John Yeamans and a number of other Barbadians, sailed for Bermuda.

About 9 December bad weather forced the vessels to put into Nevis and, during the brief stay there, it was arranged that the *Port Royal* should sail directly for Carolina and the other two vessels continue by way of Bermuda.

The three vessels were taking the same course northward before separating when disaster struck yet again, and they were scattered by another storm. The *Port Royal* was wrecked in the Bahamas and the *Three Brothers* was driven northwards to Virginia. On 12 January 1669/70 the *Carolina* struggled alone into Bermuda.

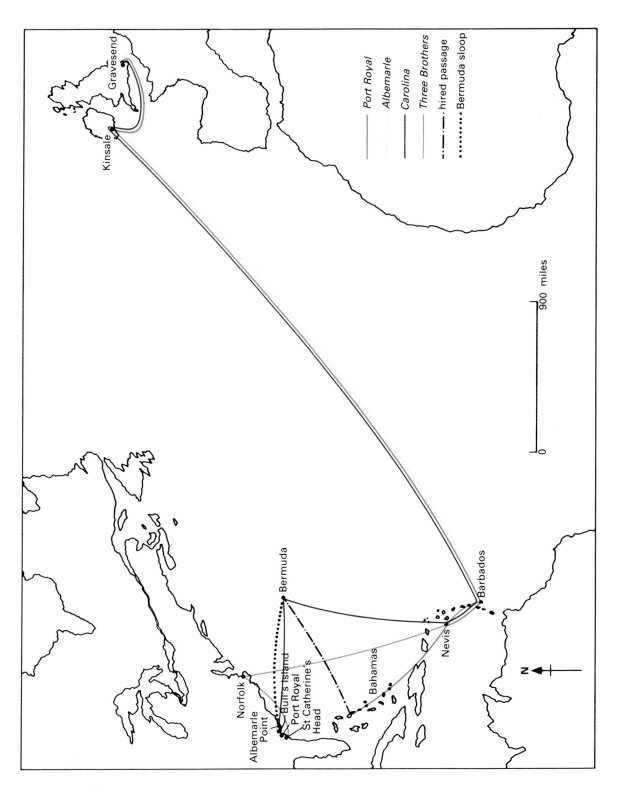

The route of the
'odyssey'

Sir John Yeamans had been granted the option either of assuming the governorship himself, or of appointing someone else in his place. At Bermuda, Yeamans inserted the name of Colonel William Sayle in the Commission. Having thus appointed Sayle Governor of Carolina, he returned once more to Barbados.

After Colonel Sayle had replaced the vessel lost in the Bahamas, he took command of the expedition and sailed, on 26 February, on the last leg of this odyssey. Before reaching Port Royal, the party landed in the middle of March at what is now Bull's Island. There the Indians gave them a friendly welcome, and the Cassique of Kiawah, who four years earlier had persuaded Colonel Sandford to visit his territory, now invited Governor Sayle to consider settling at Kiawah.

After exploring the coast southward to Port Royal, the settlers decided in favour of the Kiawah country. Early in April, almost nine months after leaving England, they landed on the west bank of the river that Sandford had named the Ashley. The spot seemed a good site for settlement, and it was named Albemarle Point in honour of the Duke of Albemarle.

On 23 May, the Barbadian sloop, *Three Brothers*, which had been driven north to Virginia, arrived at last at the settlement. Those on board had further tales of misfortune and near tragedy. On making their way south to Port Royal they overshot that harbour and made a landing instead at St Catherine Island, off the coast of what is now Georgia, on 15 May. There the Spaniards and Indians proved hostile, took several of their party prisoner and attacked the ship itself. While anchored further south five days later, they were informed by friendly Indians that the rest of the expedition had settled at Kiawah.

4
The Settlement of Charleston

The designation Charles Towne was applied to the new settlement at Albemarle Point by Lord Ashley in a letter of 1 November 1670. The settlement also gained formality in other ways. With the threat of attack by the Spaniards ever present, security naturally became the chief concern of the settlers, and fortification was given priority over such matters as town planning.

The Lords Proprietors must have been aware of the difficulty of instituting their grand model of government in so small a colony, but they wanted to have an administration based as nearly as possible on the Fundamental Constitutions. On being appointed governor, Colonel Sayle was therefore instructed to form an administration along the following lines.

He was to summon the freemen to elect five persons who, together with the five deputies appointed by the Lords Proprietors, were to form his Council; and whatever was found practicable in the Fundamental Constitutions was to be observed. Sayle was also to summon the freeholders to elect 20 persons who, together with those deputed by the Proprietors, were to form a Parliament. This body would have the power to make laws, although any such laws would be subject to ratification.

That summer, the first public elections were held for membership in the Council.

The number of Barbadians who had joined the odyssey to Carolina seems to have been relatively small. They were apparently mindful of the failure of the first settlement at Cape Fear. However, the settlers at Albemarle Point – the first Charles Town – as well as the Lords Proprietors were confident that substantial numbers of Barbadians would soon join them. As it turned out, they were not to be disappointed.

Early Public Relations Efforts

On 4 November 1670, as a result of 'intelligence' brought from Carolina by Captain Henry Brayne of the *Carolina* frigate, a proclamation was issued in Barbados extolling the wonderful conditions that were being enjoyed by the settlers. They were settled, declared this proclamation, 'in a very rich and fertile soyle', which yielded crops of such variety and abundance that there was no want of provisions. Moreover, the neighbouring Indians were so friendly that not only did they supply the settlers with much fish and game at trifling cost, but they also assisted them in clearing and cultivating their land.

The 'Barbados Proclamation' then announced that with the object of accelerating the settlement of the province and encouraging 'all manner of people who desired to transport themselves together with their servants, Negroes or utensils', the Lords Proprietors had provided the *Carolina* frigate for their transportation and that the vessel would be ready to sail in 30 days.

It was further stated that all those who had formerly underwritten 1,000 pounds (weight) or more of muscovado sugar towards defraying the cost of the Captain Hilton expedition (in 1663), would have land reserved for them. Those unable to pay their passage or furnish themselves with provisions for the voyage would have everything supplied, conditional upon their undertaking to pay the Lords Proprietors within two years 'the sume of 500 pounds of merchantable tobacco, cotton, ginger, or whatever they shall first produce'. All such (other) persons as were able to 'put in their production and other necessaries' were to pay only 100 pounds weight of muscovado sugar in Barbados, or 200 pounds weight of cotton, ginger, or tobacco in Carolina within two years.

Prospective settlers were instructed to get in touch with the merchant John Strode of St Michael's Town (Bridgetown), where, they were told, Captain Brayne would be available to confirm their agreement.

They were informed of the various land grants the Proprietors had made available: 'To every freeman that shall arrive there to plant and inhabit before the 25 March 1672, 100 acres to him and his heirs for ever; and 100 acres more to every man servant he brings with him or cause to be transported into the colony'. There were also to be 70 acres for every woman or man servant under 16 years of age, and for every servant arriving before 25 March 1672 there was to be a similar grant of 70 acres allocated when their time expired.

The *Carolina* returned to the settlement on the Ashley River early in 1671, bringing some 64 new settlers from Barbados. She was soon followed by the *John and Thomas* bringing 42 more, and during the rest of that year and for most of 1672, a number of planters moved to Carolina, taking their servants and slaves.

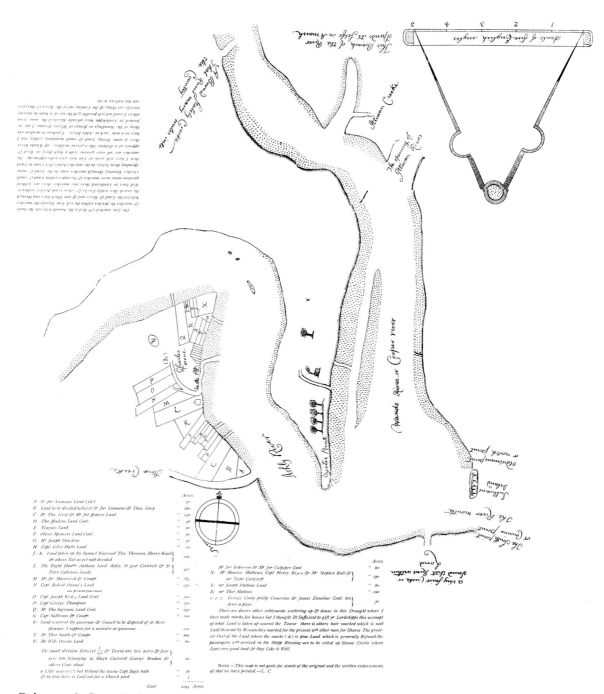

Culpepper's *Draught of the Ashley River*, 1671. Many entries are upside-down because the surveyor turned the chart as he wrote them in. (*Charleston Library Society*)

16

Even as the colonists were consolidating their settlement at Albemarle Point, Governor Sayle was considering the possibility of moving to a better location at Oyster Point, the peninsula lying between the Ashley and the Cooper Rivers. In January 1671, less than a year after the first landing, the potential of this place as the best site for a new port town was reported to Lord Ashley.

The following May the Lords Proprietors directed that, when the town was chosen, the Surveyor was to lay out the streets according to a model they had enclosed. And they further directed that.

'Those persons afterwards building were to set their houses fronting the streets so that when the town should come to be built with good houses, the streets may also be large, convenient and regular ...'

Governor William Sayle meanwhile had died in March of that year, 1671, having nomimated Joseph West as his interim successor. Then Sir John Yeamans arrived from Barbados in the summer with 50 new settlers. In April he had been made a Landgrave by the Lords Proprietors—the first inhabitant of the Province to be granted that rank of nobility. Being now the highest ranking man in the colony, he claimed his right to be governor, under the provisions of the Fundamental Constitutions.

In April 1672 he was commissioned by the Lords Proprietors, and assumed the governorship. However, his administration proved unpopular. During the first two years the Colony's food supply ran dangerously low, and disorder threatened. Yeamans' solution was to import more food on the Proprietors' account and sell it to the settlers on credit. The Proprietors blamed him for the increasing debt and accused him of profiteering on the supplies he sold to the colonists. They also accused him of having tried to reduce the authority of the proprietary deputies.

In 1674, dissatisfied altogether with his Yeaman's administration, they replaced him with Joseph West, whom they had raised to the dignity of Landgrave. But when the news reached Carolina it was only to find that Sir John Yeamans had not long died and that the Council had already elected West Governor.

During West's administration (1674–82) West remained 'undisturbed', while the Barbadians dominated both the Council and Parliament. But the Proprietors became increasingly disgusted with the provincial government because their instructions were repeatedly ignored. As Sirmans tells us, the Proprietors' discontent centred on three issues: the repayment of debts due to them, the distribution of land, and the conduct of Indian affairs (the Proprietors were opposed to the trade in Indian slaves). In 1682 West was dismissed for reportedly being involved in the Indian slave traffic.

The next governor, Sir Richard Kyrle, died shortly after arriving in the Colony (1684) and West was re-appointed. But he resigned the following year and left the Colony.

Charles Towne shown
on *A New Map of
Carolina*, Philip Lea,
1682 (*Charleston Library
Society*)

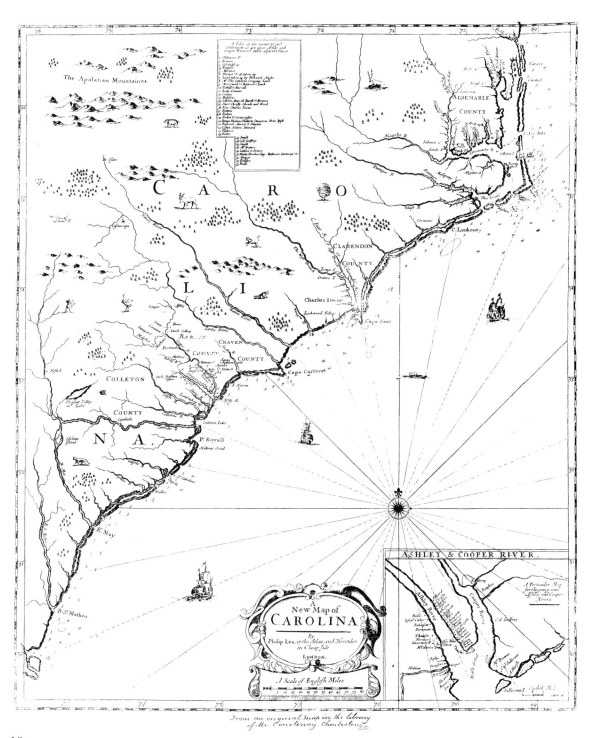

An undated plan of
Charles Town (*Library
of Congress, Washington
DC*)

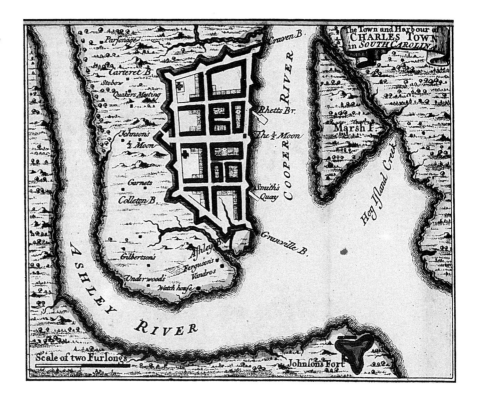

The New Town at Oyster Point

So both Yeamans and West were involved in the development of the
new port town. When Yeamans was commissioned, the Lords Proprietors had recommended that he should proceed with laying it out.
Accordingly, in July 1672, he ordered John Culpeper, the Surveyor-
General (another Barbadian) to 'admeasure and lay out for a town on
the Oyster Point'.

The area delineated was not very extensive, and initially little enthusiasm was shown by the settlers for occupying the new town. But
finally, in December 1679 during West's second term, the Lords Proprietors ordered settlement to be transferred from Albemarle Point to
the new site, which was to be the new Charles Town.

Following the exodus from the old Charles Town, the new town
began to develop rapidly, and in an account published in 1682 one
visitor reported: '... The town is regularly laid out into large and
capacious streets, which to Buildings is a great Ornament and Beauty.
In it they have reserved convenient places for Building of a Church,
Town House, and other publick Structures, an Artillery Ground for the
Exercise of their Militia, and Wharfs for the Convenience of their
Trade and Shipping.'

On its incorporation in August 1783 the town's name was changed
to Charleston, but spellings varied for some time.

19

5

The Barbadians in South Carolina

The Goose Greek Men

By 1671 immigrants from Barbados comprised about half the settler population of South Carolina. They were all too aware of their predominance in numbers, and they soon showed a desire to control the provincial government. 'The Barbadians endeavour to rule all', wrote proprietary deputy, John Coming to Sir Peter Colleton in November 1671.

In his political history of South Carolina covering the period 1663–1763, M. Eugene Sirmans (1966) tells of the impact these men had upon early Carolina:

> 'The Barbadians ... were ambitious, experienced, and occasionally unscrupulous men who had little interest in Lord Ashley's dream of erecting a perfect society in Carolina. Trained in the island colony to be enterprising and self-reliant, they were primarily concerned with making their own fortunes. They held (Governor) West and the other proprietary agents who had come from England in contempt, regarding them as inexperienced men who were unfit to manage a colony.'

During the first decade of settlement they succeeded in gaining control of the provincial government and were able to determine the course of South Carolina's politics for nearly half a century. They were concentrated near Goose Creek, a tributary of the Cooper River, and on that account acquired the designation 'the Goose Creek Men'.

Throughout the rest of the seventeenth century, Sirmans informs us, they consistently opposed proprietary policy, especially as regards religious tolerance. Staunch members of the Church of England, 'by law established', they had no sympathy for religious dissenters of any kind—an attitude that bred the factionalism which rent the colony in the 1690s.

Some of the Barbadians reputedly also engaged in practices the Proprietors condemned, particularly an Indian slave trade and a trade with pirates!

After taking office as Governor in 1686, James Colleton of Barbados, the younger brother of Sir Peter, took determined action to stamp out these practices, and succeeded in suppressing the trade with pirates, if nothing else. But Colleton was an administrator rather than a politician, and he proved no match for the powerful Goose Creek men who controlled the Carolina parliament and opposed his policies. Their opportunity to get rid of him came in 1690, when Seth Sothell, who had purchased the Clarendon proprietorship, arrived in Carolina. As a Proprietor he was senior in rank to Colleton and could claim the governorship; and backed by the Goose Creek faction he did precisely that.

Colleton and the Council contested Sothell's claim even to the point of threatening armed resistance; but Colleton was deposed bloodlessly and expelled. He returned to Barbados, where he sat in the House of Assembly from 1694 to 1701, becoming Speaker (1700–1701). He died in January 1706.

Sirmans informs us that the Lords Proprietors tried repeatedly to break the power of the Goose Creek men by replacing them with religious dissenters and other proprietary men; but all their attempts failed and they were forced to compromise.

Apart from politics, the Barbadians exercised other influences that were to have a more far-reaching effect on the social development of South Carolina. In Barbados the social order was based on slavery, and the planters who migrated to South Carolina took their slaves with them. To all intents the province became established as an off-shoot of Barbados, and these earliest immigrants, both white and black, impressed a decidedly Barbadian image on the struggling Carolina colony.

Curiously, however, although since 1668 Barbados had statutorily defined slaves as real estate, Carolina at first had no comprehensive legislation defining their legal status. When in 1690 a statute based on the Barbadian model was at last enacted, it was disallowed by the Lords Proprietors.

But the situation soon changed. By the middle of the 1690s, rice cultivation had become South Carolina's principal source of wealth. As it needed a large labour force, slaves were being imported in large numbers, especially from Madagascar and regions of West Africa where the people were familiar with the cultivation of rice. Soon the slave population was so great that it came to be regarded as a potential danger, and action was taken to regulate the management of slaves.

Once again Barbados was to provide a model. Since 1688 a law had been in force in the island which imposed severe restrictions on the personal movements of slaves, and prescribed a variety of cruel punishments, including branding in the face with a hot iron for any slave who offered even the slightest resistance to a 'Christian'—the term usually applied to any white person. In 1696 the South Carolina Assembly passed a law that was virtually a duplicate of this Act.

Then there was the matter of religion. The Goose Creek Men, as has been stated, were staunch Anglicans and firmly opposed to the religious freedom envisaged in Lord Ashley's Fundamental Constitutions. By 1700 they had organised themselves as the Church party under the leadership of Sir Nathaniel Johnson and others, and in 1704, the year after Johnson became Governor, he and his fellow Anglicans in the Assembly squeezed through a statute which excluded Dissenters from the Assembly.

The Barbadian Model

Finally, in November 1706, by another statute, the Church of England was established in the Province. Ten parishes were laid out; and it is noteworthy that six of them were named after the parishes in Barbados of St Philip, Christ Church, St Thomas, St John, St James, and St Andrew. An Anglican church was to be built in each at public expense. Later, two more parishes were created and these were also given names adopted from Barbados. In 1717 the parish of St George, Dorchester, was carved out of St Andrew, and in 1751 St Michael was created in Charles Town – later Charleston – by dividing St Philip into two.

Following the Barbadian pattern, the churchwardens and vestries of these parishes were invested with civil as well as ecclesiastical duties. In 1716 the Carolina Assembly, again using Barbados as their model, passed an Act which designated the parishes as the units for representation in the Assembly, instead of the Counties. Although this Act was disallowed in England, the settlers continued to vote by parishes until the American Revolution in 1776.

Now who were these men who so effectively transplanted Barbadian culture into South Carolina, including the plantation system, which in time would spread into other areas of the American South?

Besides the leaders, Sir John Yeamans and Sir Peter Colleton, they bore names like Middleton, Drayton, Quintyne, Daniell, Godfrey, Portman, Ledson, Maverick, Hall, Lake, Gibbes, Skene, Foster, and Schenkingh, to mention some of the more outstanding. Many were members of either the Provincial Grand Council or the Commons House of Assembly, or both. Several had been proprietary deputies, and between 1672 and 1730 eight Governors and Deputy Governors of South Carolina were men of Barbadian origin or immediate descent.

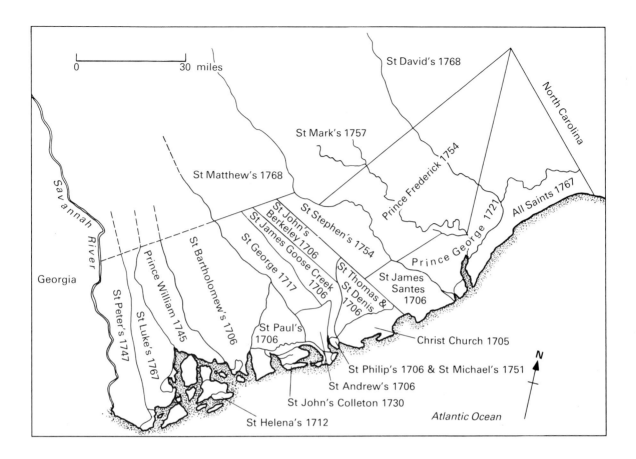

The parishes of South
Carolina, 1770,
compiled by
Historical Records
Survey, W.P.A., 1938

The Ties That Bind

For many years after the Province had been established the South
Carolinians of Barbadian descent never forgot their links with the
island. It is interesting to note that soon after about half the city of
Charles Town was destroyed by fire in November 1740, the Lieutenant
Governor, William Bull, sent a letter asking the Barbados Government
to appeal to the island's many wealthy inhabitants 'to bestow some
part of their abundance toward the relief of their suffering neighbours'.

The letter aroused a great deal of sympathy when it was read before
the island's Council, and the Acting Governor, the Honourable Ralph
Weekes, at once issued an order for special collections to be taken at
the parish churches after the Sunday Services. When this proved in-
effective, collections were taken from house to house. The money
accumulated was duly forwarded to Charles Town.

The generosity of the people of Barbados was never forgotten, and
when Bridgetown in its turn was almost totally devastated in 1766 by
two fires, the Government of South Carolina sent £785 sterling to
Barbados for charitable relief. The money was spent in due course on
the digging of wells at various points throughout Bridgetown.

6
Stede Bonnet—
Barbadian Pirate

Piracy along the Carolina coast began making an appearance not long after the colony was founded. Directed as it was against Spanish shipping, it was regarded with favour by the colonists since it helped to dampen the enthusiasm of the Spaniards for attacking the Charles Town settlement. Many of the colonists – particularly the Barbadians – reputedly also found piracy profitable! Pirates put into Charles Town to buy supplies, paying in Spanish gold and silver, and generally sold their ill-gotten goods at bargain prices.

The Lords Proprietors were opposed to this trade, however, and so was the Crown. Toward the end of the century, when piracy had reached a point where it threatened English and colonial trade, the British Parliament enacted a stringent law authorising trial of pirates in the colonies or at sea instead of transporting them to England for trial by the High Court of the Admiralty.

During the long War of the Spanish Succession (1702–13) called, in America, Queen Anne's War, piracy virtually disappeared in the region, for the sea-rovers all took to privateering against the Spaniards. The peace that followed in 1713, however, soon produced a violent resurgence of piracy when hundreds of seamen found themselves without employment. Many who had made a livelihood from the legal plundering of Spanish shipping now turned their hands to the illegal plundering of the shipping of every nationality.

The valuable cargoes entering and leaving the port of Charles Town formed a special attraction for these freebooters, and ruin threatened the trade of the city. The South Carolina Government, preoccupied with a conflict with certain Indian tribes and with the economic problems arising out of it, was unequal to the danger that came from the sea, and the loss of shipping continued.

One particular incident serves to exemplify both the insolence of the pirates and the helplessness of the authorities. A particularly infamous pirate was Edward Teach, who was better known as Blackbeard from

Stede Bonnet—
gentleman pirate
(*Library of Congress,
Washington, DC*)

an enormous black beard he had cultivated to demoralise his opponents. In May 1718 he appeared off Charles Town with a squadron of five vessels and blockaded the port for a whole week, seizing every ship entering and leaving. Among the many taken and held hostage, one especially valuable prisoner was Samuel Wragg, a member of the Provincial Grand Council, who had been bound for London. Finding himself seriously short of medical supplies, Teach arrogantly sent several of his men ashore with a message demanding a consignment from the government and threatening to murder Samuel Wragg and the other hostages if this was not forthcoming. The Governor, Robert Johnson, was forced to comply in order to save the lives of the prisoners.

Blackbeard's chief collaborator in these acts of piracy and blackmail was a certain Major Stede Bonnet, an enterprising and at first respectable native of Barbados.

Born a Gentleman

Stede Bonnet was born in 1688 and baptised in July in the Christ Church parish church. He and his two sisters were orphaned quite early in life—their father, Edward Bonnet, having died in 1694, and their mother, apparently, not long afterwards. Stede inherited his father's plantation (now called Upton) three miles east of Bridgetown. As his father had intended, his guardians brought him up as a gentleman and provided him with a 'liberal' education.

In 1709, at the age of 21, he married Mary Allamby, the daughter of a planter of St Thomas parish. The couple took up residence just 'over the bridge' at Bridgetown, and in due course became the parents of three sons and a daughter. As the owner of not less than 100 acres of land, Stede Bonnet automatically became a Major in the island's militia, as guaranteed by law. He involved himself in public affairs, and generally achieved such a reputation as an outstanding citizen that in January 1716 he was made a Justice of the Peace.

Early the following year (at the age of 29), Major Bonnet announced his intention of going abroad, and on 25 March, he drew up a legal document conferring Powers of Attorney upon his wife and two of his friends, authorising them to manage his affairs during his absence. To all appearances he was leaving on legitimate business. What they did not know was that he had secretly bought himself a sloop, named her the *Revenge*, and provided her with an armament of ten guns and a crew of 70 hands. He was about to embark upon a career of piracy on the high seas!

Now piracy was not a calling thought likely to attract such a well educated gentleman of means; so it is not surprising that, when Bonnet's friends and acquaintances heard of his criminal activities, they promptly attributed these to a mental disorder they claimed to have noticed developing on account of marital troubles. But whether he had been impelled by an unhappy marriage, or purely by a thirst for a life of adventure, one thing was certain: Major Bonnet was totally unqualified for the career he had assumed; for he lacked the most elementary knowledge of seamanship and he had to rely on the experience of his crew.

Rather surprisingly, however, he met with astonishing success on his first cruise, for off Virginia and Charles Town he captured and plundered several ships. At least two of these belonged to his native Barbados, and he took the precaution of burning them to prevent news of his pirating from being taken back to the island!

Partners in Crime

Stede Bonnet was back in the Caribbean seeking further prey when he encountered the *Queen Anne's Revenge*, commanded by the archpirate Edward Teach. After exchanging the courtesies customary among the brethren of the Black Flag, the two men agreed to work together; and Bonnet, who had assumed the name Captain Edwards, was soon engaged with his partner in plundering shipping in the West Indies. On one occasion they even raided and burnt a settlement on the French Island of Guadeloupe.

But Teach was not slow to realise that Bonnet was nothing but a novice in matters connected with the sea. He preferred to see Bonnet's sloop, the *Revenge*, in professional hands so, putting one of his own men in charge, he 'gently' persuaded Bonnet to take a cabin on board the *Queen Anne's Revenge*. Here, he assured him, he would be an honoured guest, free of the rigours and responsibilities of commanding a vessel and a crew of rough hands!

It was a successful cruise to the Bay of Honduras and a call at Grand Cayman island that enabled Teach to increase his command to the five vessels used for the blockade of Charles Town in May 1718, as already described.

For some time he had been scheming to disband his squadron and cheat all except a chosen few of his associates of their shares of the accumulated loot. He sailed to Topsail Inlet (now Beaufort Inlet), North Carolina, where by cleverly contrived 'accidents' he wrecked three of the vessels including his own ship the *Queen Anne's Revenge*. He then restored Bonnet to the command of his own sloop, the *Revenge*, and took charge of the remaining vessel himself. He calmly announced his intention of proceeding to Bath Town (now Bath) to claim the Royal Amnesty that had lately been proclaimed for all pirates who surrendered by a given date.

Stede Bonnet decided to do the same, and made his way overland to Bath Town, where the authorities gave him a certificate of pardon. When he returned to Topsail Inlet, expecting to receive his share of the plunder the company had accumulated, he was chagrined to find that Teach had absconded with everything. Enraged at the way he had been cheated, Bonnet sailed off in search of his unscrupulous partner, but failed to find him.

It was about this time that war broke out in Europe, with Spain on one side and the Triple Alliance of England, France, and Holland on the other. Bonnet was again master of his own vessel and certainly now better qualified for command. He at once obtained official clearance to proceed to the island of St Thomas to secure a commission to operate as a privateer against the Spaniards. But just as he was preparing to sail, word reached him that Blackbeard's ship was lying at anchor at Ocracoke Inlet not many miles away, with only about 20 hands on board. Again Bonnet set off in pursuit, only to find that his former partner had already sailed.

After a fruitless search lasting four days, Bonnet set course for Virginia. He now discarded his plan of going to St Thomas, and returned to his former ways: attacking and plundering every vessel he met, although he had only just received the Royal pardon for his past crimes! This pardon had been issued in his real name, Stede Bonnet, so he now took the precaution of assuming the name Captain Thomas and changed the name of his sloop from *Revenge* to *Royal James*.

On 2 July 1718, off Delaware Bay, he and his crew captured the merchant sloop *Fortune*, bound from Philadelphia to Barbados with a cargo of provisions. Two days later they took the sloop *Frances*, inbound to Philadelphia from Antigua with a valuable cargo of rum and other West Indian produce. Bonnet kept both prizes and took them to the Cape Fear River, where he set his crew to work carrying out badly needed repairs to the *Royal James*.

The several weeks needed for this task proved to be his undoing, for while it was in progress word reached Charles Town that a gang of pirates was seen in the Cape Fear River. The authorities were deeply disturbed at this report, but they became even more alarmed when Charles Vane, another notorious pirate, presently appeared off Charles Town. No doubt encouraged by Blackbeard's earlier success, he similarly sent insolent demands into the town.

This time, however, the government of South Carolina was determined not to accept any more victimisation at pirate hands. Governor Robert Johnson had two vessels, the *Henry* and the *Sea Nymph*, armed and manned and placed under the command of Colonel William Rhett, and sent out after Vane. But apparently Vane had been forewarned and decided to make a hasty departure. After making a fruitless search that lasted several days, Colonel Rhett decided to sail to the Cape Fear River and investigate the rumour that pirates were lurking there.

The Capture

On the evening of 26 September Rhett's two vessels entered the river, but they soon ran on to a sandbar. As it was dark by the time the vessels were refloated, they were obliged to anchor for the night. Some distance ahead three sloops could be seen lying at anchor—the *Royal James* and her two prizes. From these Stede Bonnet, or Captain Thomas as he was calling himself, became curious about the two sloops he could see anchored down-river and sent off a party of men to make a reconnaissance. When they returned and reported what kind of vessels they were, it did not take him long to guess the reason for their presence.

Realising that he would have to fight desperately in a bid to get clear of the enemy vessels and out into the open sea, Bonnet immediately withdrew all his men who had been manning the prizes, and set all hands to work throughout the night preparing the *Royal James* for action.

During the running battle that developed the following morning, Colonel Rhett's two vessels got on either quarter of the *Royal James*; but in the excitement all navigational caution was forgotten, and all three vessels ran into shallow water and grounded. Rhett's own vessel, the *Henry*, listed in a position that exposed her deck to small arms fire from the *Royal James*, and the damage and casualties she sustained were rendered all the more bitter by the jeering taunts of the pirates.

But the arrogance of Bonnet and his crew soon changed to dismay when a rising tide refloated the *Henry*, leaving their own vessel still helplessly stranded. The *Henry* was now able to bring her guns into action, and as she manoeuvered to finish off the *Royal James*, the pirates hauled down their black colours and surrendered. Colonel Rhett was elated on discovering that their leader, Captain Thomas, was in reality the notorious Major Stede Bonnet. His victory, however, was costly, for he had lost 18 of his men, including several who died of wounds after the action. The pirates, on the other hand, lost seven men killed outright, and two of their five wounded died later.

Bonnet and 33 surviving members of his crew were taken to Charles Town. As there was no prison, the men were placed under guard in the Watch-house; but the authorities regarded the Major as a gentleman and had him lodged in the house of the Provost Marshal, Captain Nathaniel Partridge. On the night of 24 October he escaped custody, apparently with the connivance of his guards. Whether the Provost Marshal, a Barbadian like Bonnet, was also implicated is uncertain; but the circumstances were clearly 'fishy' and in any event he was held responsible and promptly dismissed from office.

On 28 October, while Bonnet was still at large, his men were arraigned before a Court of Vice Admiralty with Nicholas Trott, South Carolina's Chief Justice, presiding. They had been indicted on two charges. One was that on the second day of August in the fifth year of the reign of His Majesty, King George the First (1718), 'they did piratically and feloniously set upon, break, board and enter a certain merchant sloop called the *Frances*, and did put her commander, Peter Mainwaring, and his mariners in corporal fear of their lives; and piratically and feloniously did steal, take, and carry away the said merchant sloop, the *Frances*, with 26 hogsheads, three tierces and three barrels of rum valued at 263 pounds, 6 shillings and 3 pence; and other goods valued at 500 pounds.'

In the second charge they were similarly accused of seizing 'in a piratical and felonious manner' the sloop *Fortune*, commanded by Captain Thomas Read, with her cargo of bread, linseed oil, hams, flour and other goods.

7

The Middletons and Middleton Place

One of the great families of South Carolina – and indeed of America – which appears to have had close links with Barbados was the Middleton family.

The founder of this family, which distinguished itself in the historical development of the Province – later the State – of South Carolina and of the United States itself was Edward Middleton, who reputedly migrated from Barbados in 1678.

Edward was the second of the three sons of Henry Middleton of Twickenham, Middlesex, England. The eldest was Arthur, also closely associated with early Carolina.

It is uncertain when Arthur Middleton migrated to Barbados and went into business, as a merchant. It is, however, on record that in 1676, together with two business associates, Arthur Middleton instituted a legal action against Edwyn Stede, the local agent of the Royal Africa Company, who had seized the *Anne*, a vessel belonging to them. Apparently she had been seized because she was an 'interloper' (a vessel trading illicitly in slaves) in infringement of the Royal Africa Company's monopoly. (One of Arthur Middleton's two associates in this affair was Bernard Schenkingh, who later achieved prominence in the political affairs of South Carolina.)

Edward Middleton reputedly also migrated to Carolina from Barbados in 1678, but his connection with the island is less clearly established. It seems unlikely that he lived there for very long before he left for Carolina, where Arthur followed in the next year, 1679.

Both brothers received large grants of land and soon became active in public affairs. Edward was appointed a deputy to the Lords Proprietors, and an Assistant Justice. In 1680 Arthur too was appointed a proprietary deputy, and held a seat on the Grand Council until 1684. At the time of his marriage in 1682 to Mary Smith, a widow, he was the owner of a plantation of some 1,780 acres. In 1683 he received a further grant of 800 acres from the Lords Proprietors as a reward for certain experiments he had made 'with oil and cotton'. He died in 1685 leaving his entire estate to his widow.

Edward Middleton had been married in England, and had a son, Henry, who became a London merchant. In Carolina, in 1680, having been a widower for some time, he married Sarah Fowell, the widow of Richard Fowell, a merchant of Barbados. This marriage produced one son, Arthur, who was the first in a long line of distinguished descendants of Edward Middleton.

The Hon. Arthur Middleton, born in 1681, was destined to outshine both his father and his uncle. By 1737, the year of his death, he had held an extensive variety of public offices and appointments, including that of Governor of South Carolina (1725–30), and in 1719 he played a leading role in overthrowing the rule of the Lords Proprietors and establishing that of the Crown.

In 1714, under the will of his father's sister, Hester Browning, the widow of Daniel Browning of Crowfield Hall, Suffolk, England, he inherited an estate in Barbados. He spent some time in the island in early 1717 visiting his property, and on 24 May, shortly before returning to South Carolina, he appointed one Thomas Palmer to be his attorney. He is thought to have visited Barbados again in 1727.

Two other Middletons who achieved national distinction in American history were Henry (1717–1784), the second son of Governor Arthur Middleton, and Henry's eldest son, Arthur (1742–1787).

The Hon. Henry Middleton, Speaker of the Commons of South Carolina, Member and President of His Majesty's Council for South Carolina, Member and President of the Provincial Congress, was a delegate to the First Continental Congress, convened in 1774, which prepared the way for the American Revolution. He served as its second president. The owner of some 50,000 acres in South Carolina, he also owned 'large estates' in Barbados and in England.

The political career of his son, the Hon. Arthur Middleton, was in several respects similar to his own, including membership of the Commons of South Carolina, the Provincial Congress and the Continental Congress. Arthur had the distinction, however, of being one of the signers of America's Declaration of Independence in 1776. In turn, his eldest son, the Hon. Henry Middleton, born in 1770, also became a member of the United States Congress and Minister to Russia.

Middleton Place

The original seat of the Middleton family was The Oaks in Berkeley County. Later we find The Oaks mentioned jointly with Crowfield, then with Middleton Place, and finally just Middleton Place.

Middleton Place,
Charleston
(Henry Fraser)

Middleton Place, 14 miles northwest of Charleston, was first settled in the late 17th century, and was acquired by Henry Middleton through marriage in 1741. The landscaped gardens, laid out by him that same year, are the oldest formal gardens in America.

The present Middleton Place House was originally built in 1755 in Georgian style, as 'a gentlemen's guest wing', flanking the main house on its southern side, while a northern flanker was built as a library. The property, like numerous others, was a victim of the Civil War (1861–1865). The south wing was restored in the 1870s, and it alone survived the earthquake of 1886 which finally destroyed the gutted walls of the main house. In the 1920s it was restored again as a family residence, but embellished with Jacobean period Dutch gables, by Mr JJ Pringle Smith, a direct descendant of Henry Middleton.

Today Middleton Place houses an impressive collection of relics of the Middleton family, including silver, family portraits, furniture, books and many items that together provide an eloquent interpretation of the family's history from 1741 to 1865. Arthur Middleton was a particularly cultured man—he had studied at Cambridge and the Middle Temple and travelled extensively in Europe. His taste in the arts was highly developed, and the artefacts reflect this taste. In the drawing room, for example, there is a Benjamin West portrait of Arthur and Mary Izard Middleton, with their infant son, Henry, in London. (Benjamin West, 1738–1820, was the celebrated and much sought after American artist who became president of London's Royal Academy. A West painting, *The Resurrection* (1776) hangs in St George's

Church, Barbados—it was a gift of the Hon. Henry Frere, President of the Barbadian Legislative Council. It is of considerable interest not only as a magnificent painting but because while it was stored in a plantation building the centurion in the painting was mistaken by a burglar for a live observer, and his eye was pierced with a dagger!)

The house was lavishly furnished, as the surviving furniture and paintings show. The library in the northern flanker contained some 12,000 volumes—many treasures survive, including a silk copy of the Declaration of Independence.

The Gardens

But the magnificence of Middleton Place is its unique garden. Begun by Henry Middleton in 1741, it is not as old as Magnolia, but it was conceived in a grand manner that is unrivalled in North America. Its wide-sweeping terraces, artificial butterfly-shaped lakes, walks and vistas over the river are breath-taking, and the small gardens and magnificent trees complete what was once described as 'This premier garden of the thirteen colonies'. The Middleton Oak has a circumference of 30 feet and is thought to be more than a thousand years old.

Arthur's son (the second Henry Middleton) enlarged his grandfather's garden. André Michaux, the famous French botanist, visited Middleton Place, bringing some of the first camelias to be planted in

Middleton Place—aerial view of the butterfly lakes (*N. Jane Iseley, c/o Middleton Place*)

an American garden. The Library contains a copy of Thomas Walters'
Flora Caroliniana (1788) in which Henry inscribed 'This was Michaux's
copy'.

Henry's son, William introduced the azalea. Ironically, William
signed the Ordinance of Secession and so destroyed the Union his
family had struggled for.

Middleton Place is now a registered National Historic Landmark. It
is owned by the Middleton Place Foundation, a non-profit public trust
established in 1975 and administered by a small professional staff. The
house, gardens and restored plantation stable yards are open to the
public under the aegis of the Foundation. They provide a superb
example of a living, thriving antebellum plantation at work as it was
200 years ago.

8
Sir John Yeamans and St Nicholas Abbey

What spirit of adventure and perhaps recklessness moves the world's great pioneers? Sir John Yeamans, first Governor-designate and third Governor of Carolina, certainly led an adventurous life but his colourful career, his political expediency in changing from Royalist to Commonwealth supporter and back to Royalist (with a baronetcy), his affair with and marriage to the wife of his business partner, Colonel Benjamin Berringer, and the scandal surrounding Berringer's death all suggest that Yeamans was quite a character. For about ten years he must have lived with his new wife Margaret Berringer at St Nicholas Abbey (then Berringer's). It was a mansion house as dramatic, colourful and mysterious as this man himself, Sir John Yeamans, who perhaps more than anyone else personified the ruthless spirit of

St Nicholas Abbey in the parish of St Peter, Barbados (circa 1660): east front (*Henry Fraser*)

opportunism of the seventeenth century Caribbean arena.

Yeamans was the son of a Bristol brewer, and must have set sail for Barbados as a very young man, for in 1638 he was already listed as owner of more than ten acres. By 1641 he was joint landowner with Benjamin Berringer of land in St Peter and St Andrew, and in 1643 the two men were living together on the same plantation. They appear to have been real estate speculators and developers of agricultural lands.

Both Yeamans and Berringer were Councillors and Royalists. When Barbados capitulated to the Commonwealth expedition in January 1652, Yeamans was able to 'accommodate to the new regime' (Campbell, 1986) and was again a Member of the Assembly by 1655.

Berringer retired from public life and appears to have gone to England from 1652 to 1656. He left his wife Margaret, daughter of the Reverend John Forster, behind. He then returned and lived at what is now St Nicholas Abbey until his sudden death in January 1661. But no doubt his long absence led to the inevitable—marital infidelity. Although his wife bore him three more children after 1656, it was agreed 'that she behaved abominably to her husband for a long time before his death and it was obvious that she had transferred her affections to John Yeamans,' (witnesses at the inquiry into Berringer's will, quoted by Campbell). It seems that Berringer was often so exasperated that he would leave the matrimonial home to stay with friends.

On the last such occasion at a house in Speightstown he died and it seems clear from documents recently discovered (Campbell) that Berringer's death was procured, presumably by poisoning, by Yeamans, 'for no other reason but that he had a mind to the other gentleman's wife', as Governor William Lord Willoughby put it in a report of 1668.

By this time Yeamans had been created a baronet, designated Lieutenant-General and Governor of Carolina and led an expedition of the 'Adventurers' to explore Carolina. He was intended to be Governor of the settlers who eventually made it to Charleston in 1670, but as we know he nominated octogenarian Colonel William Sayle of Bermuda in his place, and returned to the home comforts of Lady Margaret. But perhaps Lady Margaret was being unfaithful again or he was just restless, for by 1671 he was in Charleston, agitating for the Governorship. When he became Governor in 1672 a major task was the laying out of the final site of Charleston at Oyster Point, so perhaps it was he, Yeamans, who transported Broad Street, Barbados to Broad Street, Charleston. By 1674 he was dead.

The Inheritance of Berringer's

Colonel Berringer's plantation passed to his elder son and then to his younger son, whose daughter Susannah inherited. She married George

Nicholas, whose name the plantation acquired. By 1730 it was in debt, and sold to Joseph Dottin who bequeathed it to his daughter Christian. She married John Gay Alleyne, later Sir John, Baronet, one of the most outstanding Barbadians of any period of history. He lived there from 1746 until 1801. Tradition holds that Sir John's son, Sir Reynold Abel Alleyne, once rode a horse up the Chippendale staircase of Nicholas in pursuit of a young lady!

On Sir John's death the plantation reverted to the Dottins. (Sir John and his first wife were childless and, when ill in 1782 made a settlement of the estate on her relatives after his death. But after Lady Alleyne's death Sir John rallied long enough to marry a cousin in 1786 by whom he had seven children!)

The Dottins lost the estate in the Chancery Court in 1816 and it was bought by two Cumberbatch brothers, Edward and Lawrence. The Cumberbatch brothers lived in the parish of St Nicholas, Bristol, hence perhaps the explanation of the 'canonisation'. It has been suggested that it was on the occasion of the marriage of Lawrence's daughter Sarah Cumberbatch to Charles Cave, in Bath Abbey that the 'Abbey' was added. Lieutenant Colonel Stephen Cave, the present owner, is a direct descendant of that union—the great, great grandson of Charles and Sarah Cave.

St Nicholas Abbey:
a) North view, showing separate kitchen wing
b) Twin bath-house and communal (four-seater) toilet
c) Pineapple finial on garden pillar—common in Charleston but rare in Barbados (*Henry Fraser*)

a)

b)

c)

St Nicholas Abbey

St Nicholas Abbey is a pure Jacobean mansion transplanted into the tropics, chimneys and all. To the uninitiated the first glimpse of this superb architectural gem in its setting of tropical spendour is an extraordinary surprise.

The original facades are unaltered except for an arcaded entrance porch of three Roman arches, almost certainly an eighteenth century addition. There are three stories and three beautiful curvilinear Dutch gables, surmounted with tall finials and with unusually designed chimneys at the four corners. Clearly plans for an English mansion were followed to the letter, including unnecessary fireplaces and chimneys.

The windows and corners of the building are surrounded by elaborate quoins. The present windows are Georgian sash windows but would almost certainly have replaced original casements or mullioned windows. The 'Chinese chippendale' staircase is said to have been built for Sir John Gay Alleyne in 1746. The cedar panelling of the main reception rooms is nineteenth century. The decorative arches and mouldings are of uncertain date but certainly contemporary with late Jacobean in England. Apart from the porch and panelling and the modern plumbing and electricity the house is essentially pure and, contrary to some accounts, there is no evidence of any significant alterations to the original fabric.

Oral tradition gives St Nicholas Abbey a date of 1660. Peter Campbell (1986) debates the historical evidence and ascribes a date of 1656–1661, between Colonel Berringer's return from England and his apparent murder. Architectural evidence supports this view, for the house is a fine example of Jacobean architecture (from 1620 until the Restoration, i.e. the transition period between Tudor or Elizabethan and the Classical or Renaissance style). It is plausible for Berringer to have returned from England with the finest plans for a fashionable great house. It is unlikely that the circumstances of the estate would have permitted such a mansion to be built at any time again until Sir John Gay Alleyne moved in. By that time, at the height of the Georgian period, such a house would have been so old-fashioned that it would have been inconceivable. Indeed it is most likely that the contrasting Georgian porch and new staircase were Sir John's concessions to 'good taste' in an attempt to 'modernise' this by then ancient and 'unfashionable' great house of a past era!

The significance of such a house being built in rural Barbados by the year 1660, and surviving in such a state today, is most extraordinary. There are only two houses in the entire continent of North America which are comparable in size, Jacobean style and architectural merit. One is Drax Hall, also in Barbados, believed to have been built either by Colonel James Drax (a prominent Puritan or Republican who supported Oliver Cromwell and who pioneered sugar growing in

Drax Hall, St George, Barbados, believed built around 1653 (*Henry Fraser*)

Barbados) or more probably by his son, Henry Drax, in the 1650s. The other is Bacon's Castle in Surrey County, Virginia. Bacon's Castle was built in 1665 (not in 1655 as often stated) by Arthur Allen, a merchant and it was used as a fortress in the Bacon rebellion in 1676. Both St Nicholas and Drax Hall appear to be of slightly earlier date.

Of the three houses St Nicholas is certainly the most elegant. Both it and Drax Hall are 'double houses' with four chambers and a central hall; Drax Hall has a magnificently carved Jacobean staircase of mastic wood. Thus both are more luxurious houses than Bacon's Castle, and illustrate the great wealth that sugar was producing for the Barbadian planters by the mid-seventeenth century. One cannot but wonder if there was rivalry between the Royalist Berringer and the Republican Drax to build the finest house!

For Sir John Yeamans to leave this kind of wealth and comfort for the uncertainties of a new colony at the age of 60 seems somewhat surprising. Perhaps his sins had caught up with him, or perhaps, like Stede Bonnet he had 'marital troubles'. Or perhaps he had the restless pioneering spirit and the chance to be Governor of a great new country drove him on.

NOTE: St Nicholas Abbey is well preserved by its present owner. It is furnished in period style and is open to the public on weekdays. It is part of the annual Barbados National Trust Open House programme in the 'winter' Tourist season.

41

9
The Drayton Connection

Among the many early settlers of South Carolina who came from Barbados was Thomas Drayton, who had emigrated from London to Barbados with his father in 1675. Thomas Drayton the elder settled in the parish of St Michael, where in 1680 he owned 12 acres of land, one hired servant, one bought servant and seven slaves. This suggests a certain lack of success for someone from a family of landed proprietors in England. Lack of opportunity in 'overcrowded' Barbados must have led young Thomas to choose the new colony of Carolina, and he left Barbados on April 25, 1679 in the good ship *Mary*. He was apparently accompanied by one or more of his family's slaves, for the gatekeeper at Drayton Hall, 70 year old Richmond Bowens, claims to be an eighth generation descendant of a slave named Bowen who accompanied Thomas Drayton. (The name Bowen is strongly associated with the parish of St Lucy in Barbados.)

In the same year and on the same ship another Barbadian, Stephen Fox, also went to Charles Towne, acquiring land on the Ashley River. Thomas Drayton married Ann Fox, daughter of Stephen, and inherited this land, which was to become the nucleus of Magnolia Plantation. His son, Thomas Drayton III, (1708–1760) inherited Magnolia in turn and the now famous Magnolia Gardens have remained in the ownership of a direct line of Drayton descendants for nearly 300 years.

Thomas Drayton III's brother John (1713–1779) acquired land next door to Magnolia, also on the Ashley River. There he built Drayton Hall, between 1738 and 1742. His brother's son, William, inherited Magnolia but moved to Florida as Chief Royal Justice. John then acquired Magnolia as well.

One of his sons, Thomas, inherited Magnolia and another, Charles, inherited Drayton Hall. These two properties are justly considered two of the most remarkable sites in the United States.

Magnolia Garden, created by Thomas Drayton II (Junior), has been described as 'too beautiful to paint' (John Galsworthy) and 'Charleston's greatest treasure' (AAA Motorist, 1983). It is certainly the hemisphere's oldest major garden. It was listed by the *Baedecker Guide for America* in 1900 as one of the three sights worthy of two stars—the other two were Niagara Falls and the Grand Canyon!

Drayton Hall elicits even more extravagant admiration from architectural buffs. It has been described as America's earliest, one of the finest and probably THE finest American example of Georgian Palladian architecture; a treasure, of profound architectural significance, the most interesting early Georgian building in America, the best in Southern architecture, etc., etc. Indeed to many people it is a veritable temple of the greatest beauty, and its survival in the purest, unaltered form for 250 years is nothing short of miraculous.

The Drayton family claim to trace their descent from a Norman, Aubrey deVere, who came to England with William the Conqueror,

Magnolia House and
Gardens, Charleston,
South Carolina
(*Courtesy of Magnolia
Plantation and Gardens*)

43

and was rewarded for service with a Saxon property. His son became Lord Chief Justice to King Henry I. His grandson assumed the name of his property (Drayton) and *his* grandson Sir Walter deVere Drayton earned fame in the crusades alongside Richard I. The Drayton family also played important roles in American colonial history, but Magnolia and Drayton Hall are monuments which will inspire millions for generations to come.

Magnolia

Thomas Drayton, Junior, and his wife Ann are credited with the first major development of the Magnolia Plantation's garden, and with building the first Magnolia House. This was burnt by the British troops when they camped there during the Revolutionary War. Governor John Drayton (born 1766), who became Governor of South Carolina, described it in his memoirs as 'unquestionably one of the most ancient if not THE most ancient Mansion House in South Carolina', with ceilings eighteen feet high and ornaments of stucco work.

The second Plantation House met a similar fate, at the hands of General Sherman's troops. The present house was rebuilt by the owner of the Civil War period, Rev. John Grimke Drayton, rector of the ancient St Andrew's Episcopal Church nearby (built in 1706 and the burial site of many early Barbadian settlers). He used the bricks of his summer house 14 miles up river, transported by barge and reassembled on the foundations of the burned out house, adding further rooms and a Victorian tower in the 1880s.

The Gardens themselves encompassed 10 acres by the time Thomas Drayton died in 1717. The Plantation was inherited by the Rev. John Grimke Drayton at the age of 22. He developed it, restored it after the Civil War, and opened it to the public in 1870. Today the Plantation's entire 500 acres comprise the gloriously extended gardens within a wild-life sanctuary. It is thus America's oldest man-made tourist attraction, and is tended today with passionate care by John Drayton Hastie, ninth generation direct descendant of Thomas and Ann Drayton. Its fame rests on its magnolias, its extraordinary riot of azaleas, camellia, japonica (90 varieties), its beautiful lagoon, its giant oaks and cypresses and much else. 'None in the world is so beautiful – it is a kind of Paradise – it is other worldly'. (John Galsworthy, 1921).

Drayton Hall

Drayton Hall was built by Royal Judge John Drayton, Member of His Majesty's Council. It was begun in 1738 and completed in 1742, and the magnificence of its design and its interiors are ample testimony of

Drayton Hall,
Charleston, South
Carolina—west front
(*Henry Fraser*)

the taste and style of the man who was considered the wealthiest planter in South Carolina.

Drayton Hall has survived not only the Revolutionary War, the ravages of the Civil War, fire-risks, a major earthquake and numerous devastating hurricanes, but – more miraculously than all these – the ever-present threat of progress. For reasons unknown the Drayton family resisted the temptation to modernise—they never put in piped water, toilets, gas or electricity. The only concessions were a wood burning stove in the basement, a hand water pump on the outside and modification of the roof, while an updating of taste took place in 1803 with the introduction of three Adam mantels! From time to time new ceilings were created, and the second (and last) interior paint job was carried out in 1865—a uniform blue in the great hall and most other rooms. When the National Trust acquired it in 1974 it acquired a monument of remarkable purity.

When Drayton Hall was built the Ashley River was the easiest mode of transportation. There is a formal river front facade that 'conforms to the Palladian ideal of balance and order' (Ruth Reeves, in *Southern Accents*, 1982). The west front, overlooking the reflecting pool and flanked by curved wings and dependencies (no longer standing) is even more perfectly Palladian. A very grand two-storey pedimented portico is approached by twin flights of stairs to a marbled loggia. The great halls on the first floor and above, on the second floor, were designed for

45

lavish entertainment, and the Draytons apparently held lavish candlelit balls, with a fire truck on site and firemen dressed as footmen in every room, to be ready for any mishap.

The interiors of Drayton Hall are particularly exquisite. It is a complete expression of the concepts of order, symmetry, classical form and aesthetic harmony of Andreas Palladio. In every detail – the elaborate plaster work ceilings, the Palladian over mantel in the first floor great hall, the richly carved cornices and festoons over the windows – Drayton Hall demonstrates an achievement that antedates anything remotely comparable in America by decades. And although there are bigger and grander buildings of every major architectural style throughout the Eastern States, few would argue that Drayton Hall stands supreme in concept and execution.

The Barbadian Branch

The departure of Thomas Junior for Carolina was not surprising as his father had a large family of at least six children. The local branch of the family multiplied and married into practically every other Barbadian family—Carter, Massiah, Field, Springer, Durant, Ince, Parris, Boyce, Mahon, Fraser, etc., and at various times owned a number of plantations, including Molyneux in St James.

Perhaps the best known member of the Barbadian Draytons is Geoffrey, writer and author of *Christopher*, the poetic and evocative novel of a boy growing up in Barbados (first published 1959 and in Caribbean Writers Series, Heinemann).

10

The Charleston Single House and the Barbadian Connection

The Charleston 'Single House' has been described as 'the city's most distinctive contribution to American domestic architecture.' Indeed the Single House survives as an apparently unique creation, designed in Charleston to suit its particular situation and generating a uniquely elegant and harmonious townscape. The city has been described as 'the most civilised town in the world' and in 1986 was winner of the USA's annual City Livability Award. It owes much of its charm to the fascinating Single House, which traditionally has roots in the West Indies, and has been specifically attributed to Barbados by many writers.

But what exactly is the Single House, and is there really evidence for a connection with Barbados? Kenneth Severens of the University of Charleston describes it as a creative response to indigenous factors. These factors were the climate and the location. The situation of Charleston on the tip of a peninsula limited its expansion and resulted in long, very narrow house lots. This formal plan prevented ad hoc growth and the accommodation of personal whim in the shape and size of house lots. But the hot, humid summers did not allow typical European 'row houses'. Houses grew up instead as long, narrow, free-standing houses, allowing the breeze to blow around and through. These 'Single Houses' became dominant by the mid-eighteenth century, and examples of them can be seen on some of the old city plans and maps.

Both the oldest pre-revolutionary Single Houses and their later nineteenth century successors share certain basic features, even though some of the later versions became very grand, with the finest Georgian, Federal and Greek revival detailing.

A classic Charleston
'Single House'
(*Felix Kerr*)

The Typical Single House

Much has been written about these fascinating houses. A typical Single House is a long narrow rectangle, a single room wide and with a single gable roof. The short side or gable end faces the street. The main entrance opens centrally on the long side, into a central stairhall. This divides the interior into two rooms on each floor, plus the hallway. If there was a business on the ground floor there was always a street entrance.

Verandahs (known in Charleston as piazzas) were added on the long side, which almost invariably faced south or west to catch the summer breeze. The side opposite the piazza was placed on the lot line and in many houses virtually closed to ensure privacy, except for stair windows for ventilation. There would be a long narrow garden on the piazza side.

The piazzas have open 'colonades' but are usually closed at the street end, with an outer door to the street. The columns in the older, smaller houses are traditionally wooden posts, turned or chamfered (square in cross-section and grooved at the four corners), but attain the

A more sophisticated single house) the Edmonston-Alston House at 21 East Battery, Charleston (*Felix Kerr*)

proportions and elegance of Doric or Corinthian columns in the grander houses, such as the Edmonston-Alston House at 21 East Battery. This elegant town house was built in 1828 by Charles Edmonston and purchased soon afterwards by Charles Alston, a wealthy rice planter. It is now a fascinating house museum, open to the public. Like most of the larger Single Houses the most elegant formal entertaining rooms are on the second floor, for better ventilation (and better views—some of the most elegant houses stand on East Battery).

A Charleston carriage on the elegant East Battery surveys a highly embellished and unusually elaborate Single House (*Felix Kerr*)

The Barbadian Connection

Evidence of several kinds suggests that the Single House may well have come to Charleston from Barbados. This evidence is pictorial, historical, linguistic and architectural. Settlers brought their slaves and the cultivation of sugar from Barbados. Since Barbadians played such an integral part in the exploration of South Carolina and the settlement of Charleston, it would not be surprising to find evidence of other Barbadian influences. They certainly had an influence on the social habits, and oral tradition says that the design of the Single House came from Barbados.

However, there is, by and large, no similarity between what may be called 'main stream' or the typical traditional, vernacular architecture of Barbados, and the Single House of Charleston. This is not at all surprising, since the main influence on Caribbean architecture (and Barbados in particular) was Georgian, introduced *after* the period of strong links with Charleston, i.e. after the war of Independence. By the nineteenth century a style had evolved which was Georgian in derivation yet distinctly its own, i.e. Barbadian vernacular. If the Single House came to Charleston from Barbados, this must have happened in an earlier tradition of the seventeenth century.

Pictorial evidence

The early buildings of Bridgetown were repeatedly destroyed by a series of major fires. But we have a very good idea of their appearance from pictures, particularly a unique 1695 engraving by Samuel Copen published by J. Kip in London and to be seen in the Cunard Print Gallery of the Barbados Museum. Copen's panoramic view, *A prospect of Bridgetown in Barbados*, shows tall, narrow, gabled houses, some with Dutch gables, remarkably similar to rows of Single Houses—standing close but separate.

Strong historical and linguistic evidence comes from a remarkable book *A true and exact History of the Island of Barbados*, by Richard Ligon, first published in London in 1657. Ligon could be described as Barbados' first historian, architect, naturalist and industrial consultant! He was a Royalist supporter of King Charles I, who after Cromwell's victory in 1649, took refuge in pro-Royalist Barbados.

His book not only summarised the brief history of Barbados but detailed the flora and fauna, gave an account of sugar production with accurate plans for the 'Ingenuo' or sugar works, and gave a critical analysis of how to build for the tropics. It is this account of Ligon's 'tropical house design' which we feel may have set a pattern for seventeenth century building in Barbados and influenced the design of houses in early Charleston.

Detail of Copen print on pages 52–3, showing tall narrow houses with a single gable

Ligon wrote of 'single houses'—the only use of this term anywhere outside of Charleston. He decried the houses of those times in Barbados as being intolerably hot and uninhabitable. He described the advantages of a 'single house', as opposed to a 'double house' with two (parallel) gables, for the hot climate, and recommended how it should be aligned to reduce the full force of the sun, i.e. on an East-West line, with the shorter sides to the sun:

> 'A single house that is built long-wise, and upon a North South line, has these disadvantages. The sun shines upon the East side-walls from six o'clock till eight, so as the beam rests flat upon that side for two hours ... Whereas if you build your house upon an East and West line, you have these advantages, that in the morning the sun never shines in or near an oblique line above two hours, etc. ...
>
> 'I do confess that I love a double house, much better than a single, but if it have a double cover, that is, two gable ends

A Prospect of Bridgetown in Barbados, engraving by Samuel Copen, 1695

and a gutter between, though it be built upon an East and West line yet the sun (which must lie upon it all the heat of the day) will so multiply the heat, by reflecting the beams from inside to inside, as you shall feel that heat above too sensibly in the ground stories below, though your siding be a foot thick.'

Thus Ligon used the terms 'single' and 'double' house in a way that has survived in Charleston and Charleston alone.

Surviving seventeenth century Barbadian plantation houses such as St Nicholas Abbey and Drax Hall are typical Jacobean houses of the period with complex gable arrangements. A number of eighteenth century houses survive which are simple 'double houses', i.e. two long rectangles, placed side by side, with a supporting wall in the middle, carrying two parallel gables with a 'valley gutter' in between. There are, however, three of the most important seventeenth century plantation houses which are Single Houses in Ligon's sense of the term, i.e. a

long rectangle, a single room wide. All are disposed in an East West
line—Brighton House (1652), the Principal's Lodge, Codrington Col-
lege (c. 1670 or earlier) and the Bay Mansion, of uncertain date. They
are generously proportioned, free standing in extensive grounds and
have been added to over the years. They will not therefore be described
here although they are of great interest as they clearly began with the
basic Single House form, possibly built to Ligon's specifications.

Barbadian Single Houses

There appear, however, to be several 'Single Houses' surviving, on the
outskirts of Bridgetown, beyond the 'burnt districts', and in Speightstown. They are 'town houses', built in close relation to other houses,
and show most of the characteristics of the Charleston Single House.

The most outstanding is Arlington in Speightstown, the home of the
Skinner merchant family for several generations. This house with its
strikingly narrow vertical form, three stories, steeply pitched gabled
roof and dormer windows, could have come straight out of Copen's
engraving, and shows a remarkable resemblance to early Charleston
houses, including the flare to the lower part of the gable. It is a long,
very narrow house, a single room wide, with spacious rooms on the
upper floor entered in the middle of the long side. There were galleries
or piazzas on the garden side, removed in 1950 when the house was
acquired to become Barbados' first Public Health Clinic.

A small and almost perfect example of a Single House is Industry

Arlington, a 'Single House' in Speightstown, Barbados—probably eighteenth century (*Felix Kerr*)

Cot in Bay Street, now known as the Boatyard, a popular haven and 'watering place' for international and local yachtsmen. The stairs in the central stairhall have been removed in recent alterations and a staircase provided at the end of the house away from the street.

A third house of essentially Single House design is the historic Seaview Hotel at Hastings, near the Garrison (c. 1800). Although very close to the Garrison, and built almost entirely of brick, like most Garrison buildings which are of uniformly Georgian design, it is essentially a Single House of extremely generous proportions. Its main entrance, in the middle of the long side (garden side) is pretentious, with a large, arched doorway and heavy panelled doors, but the window and door openings conform to the common eighteenth century Barbadian vernacular, being ten to twelve inches narrower on the outside than the inside. To the right of the stairhall is a single large room on the ground floor, while to the left a corridor divides the western part of the house into smaller rooms. Verandahs (or piazzas) on both floors run along the south (long) side of the building, and on

55

Seaview Hotel, Hastings, Barbados (circa 1800), prior to 1988 restoration (*Henry Fraser*)

The Virginian Restaurant, Barbados (*Felix Kerr*)

Town house of Single House style, probably eighteenth century with later nineteenth century style verandah (*Felix Kerr*)

the upper floor at the east end. The Seaview has been a hostelry, or in Bajan parlance a Guest House, for a hundred years, and has just undergone major restoration. Its famous Virginian Restaurant next door occupies a fine example of early nineteenth century 'Bajan Georgian', splendidly restored.

Here and there in old sections of Bridgetown, in Bay Street, Roebuck and Baxter's Road, can be seen other houses of 'Single House' type, but most are considerably altered. The last great Bridgetown fire of 1860 would have wiped out most of the remaining early houses in the main, central part of the city and the extensive rebuilding was done in a uniform style, with the characteristic Georgian symmetry and Victorian detailing that characterised all Barbadian buildings for another 75 years.

Later Barbadian Architecture

Both the nineteenth century town house and the suburban villas have distinctive features that are as unique to Barbados as the Single House became to Charleston. The long, narrow shape remained, but a central axis and a symmetrical street front became the dominant features. (See 'The Book Place', a typical nineteenth century Barbadian town house, with shop entrances below and living quarters above. The ubiquitous verandah or 'gallery' was where family and friends would gather in the afternoon and watch the world go by).

'The Book Place'—a later (nineteenth century) town house in Bay Street, Bridgetown, now an antiquarian and second-hand bookshop, showing two varieties of classic overhanging verandahs (*Felix Kerr*)

Bell pelmets at
Ronald Tree House,
Belleville, Barbados
(headquarters of the
Barbados National
Trust) (*Henry Fraser*)

Villa Franca,
Hastings, Barbados—
a classic suburban
villa and site of the
first public bath
houses opened in 1836
(*Felix Kerr*)

Other details developed: jalousie windows (adjustable wooden slats to let light and breeze in but keep rain out), hooded windows and Demerara windows (long, adjustable hoods, often with fixtures at the sides and a projecting slatted shelf, known as a 'cooler window', on which plants or earthenware water jugs could be kept cool). On the small houses roofs were high pitched for coolness, with gable-end windows high up for extra ventilation, but large houses had parapets to protect them from the devastation of hurricanes.

Most of these features were devised in response to climatic conditions—the heat, the tropical downpours of rain and the sudden storms which sometimes churn through the Northeastern Caribbean in August and September. But some, like the elegant bell-shaped Bajan window hoods and the ornate wooden tracery decorating verandahs and roofs, are purely 'for style', and create what has been described as Caribbean Style, in the lavish book of that name (see bibliography).

Charming wooden chattel house at Welches Plantation, St Thomas (home of 'Best of Barbados' arts and crafts industry) (*Felix Kerr*)

Wooden suburban house in Belleville, Barbados, with multiple gabled roofs—a larger version of the chattel house (*Felix Kerr*)

Altogether, a range of traditional house forms evolved in Barbados, from the planter's mansion (built of coral stone) through town houses and suburban villas to the modest wooden 'chattel' house, so called because it was designed to be moved. These Bajan vernacular houses were the local version of a wider Caribbean architectural development (see *Caribbean Georgian*, and *Historic Houses of Barbados*), and were as unique as the Charleston Single House. They remained essentially unchanged for a hundred years, giving Bridgetown, its suburbs and the villages across Barbados a character and picturesqueness of their own.

The post war era brought a new international flavour, and 'development' has done serious damage to the architectural heritage of Barbados. Yet many features in common with Charleston have helped Barbadians in striving to preserve their heritage—economic decline (in our case the decline of sugar) and the intrinsic thriftiness of the Bajan has to some extent tempered demolition and 'overbuilding'. The work of the Barbados National Trust, founded in 1961, has done a great deal to sensitise Barbadians to the value of their historic architecture, by restoring and encouraging the restoration of important buildings and sites. Although we can point to only a few remaining Single Houses, we can boast of hundreds of plantation Great Houses, (like Villa Nova, Sunbury Plantation House Museum and Sam Lord's Castle), scores of Gothic coral stone churches, a handsome Garrison of arcaded brickwork, and a plethora of windmills, chattel houses and much more to tell the story of Barbados, gateway to Carolina and the Americas.

Harmony Hall,
St Michael, Barbados
(circa 1700), taken in
1952. Now 'Solidarity
House', headquarters
of the Barbados
Workers Union
(*Felix Kerr*)

Villa Nova, St John,
Barbados. Built in
1834 and more
recently the winter
residence of the late
Lord Avon
(Sir Anthony Eden)
(*Henry Fraser*)

Sunbury Plantation
House Museum,
St Philip, Barbados;
uncertain date—
probably late
seventeenth century
(*Henry Fraser*)

Sam Lord's Castle,
St Philip, Barbados
(now part of Marriott's
Resort), circa 1820
(*Felix Kerr*)

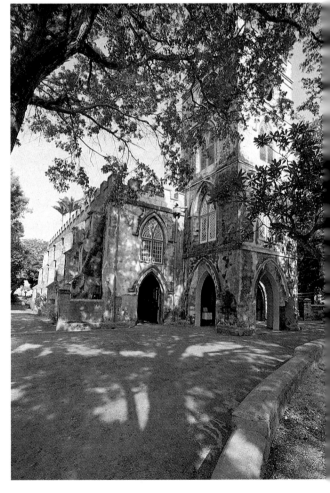

St John's Parish
Church, Barbados
(*Willie Alleyne*)

The Barbados
Museum, The
Garrison (old Military
Prison) (*Henry Fraser*)

Morgan Lewis Sugar
Windmill Museum,
St Andrew, Barbados
(preserved by the
Barbados National
Trust) (*Henry Fraser*)

Gun Hill Signal
Station, St George,
Barbados (preserved
by the Barbados
National Trust)
(*Henry Fraser*)

11

Gullah and Bajan Dialect

Barbadians visiting Charleston and Charlestonians in Barbados may be struck by a similarity of both accent and idiom in the two places. Considering the diversity of Afro-American English and of Caribbean creole English, this may seem at first a little surprising. It is not so surprising if we remember the early history of Charleston and the large numbers of Barbadians and their slaves who were among the earliest settlers. Yet the precise origin of Gullah, the creole dialect spoken in Charleston and coastal South Carolina, is highly controversial among linguists.

One school of thought, expounded by Cassidy, claims that Gullah is derived from a Barbadian creole, developed by 1670 and transplanted to Charleston in the first few decades of settlement. In fact, Barbadians (or Bajans) also emigrated in large numbers in that period to Suriname and Jamaica, and Cassidy considers that the dialects of all three countries began in Barbados and went their separate ways. This makes the resemblance between Gullah and Bajan (the present day Barbadian dialect in purest form) all the more remarkable.

The opposing view (Hancock) is that an English creole was introduced into Charleston later by slaves from the Upper Guinea coast. There seems to be little doubt that a Guinea Coast creole English existed in the seventeenth century, but there is a dearth of evidence, for or against, to say if a distinctive Barbadian creole ever developed, which could have given rise to Gullah. The relative closeness of today's Barbadian speech to Standard English, compared, for instance, to rural Jamaican, may be used as evidence against it. But it has been suggested that because Barbados is so small, and slaves lived in such proximity to the planters, any early Barbadian pidgin or creole would have been more rapidly decreolised than elsewhere, for example Jamaica. This may explain the smaller number of African words retained in Barbados in comparison with Jamaica. In fact, *unna* (you, singular), *wunna* (you, plural), *nyam* (eat), *bittle* (food), *okra* or *okry* (the green vegetable), and the game *warri* are about the only pure African words retained in Barbadian creole.

But similarities between Gullah and Bajan abound—they may be considered under many headings, but chiefly the structure of the language, pronunciation or phonology, 'expressions', and the use of proverbs. Many of the similarities are common to other Caribbean creoles – like the words *unna* and *nyam* – all that is intended here is to highlight some features which seem specific for Gullah and Bajan, which will receive more scholarly treatment from linguists elsewhere.

Structure

A few examples will suffice: for example, use of verbal adjectives abounds in both Gullah and Bajan: *I glad*, *I sad*, *I vex* (angry); failure to distinguish present and past tense, e.g. *I eat* indicates past or present, but *I eat already* makes the past tense clear, while *I does eat 'nuff* indicates a habitual or regular action ! Verb combinations, for example *he gone and done the very thing I tell him not to* are common.

In Gullah and Bajan, the active voice may be used for the passive, for example, *this fruit can eat now*. Do not be misled: this is no carnivorous fruit, but a fruit that is 'ripe enough to be eaten!'

It is a general Creole feature to ask questions without changing the order of the words but merely by a change in intonation. In Gullah the word *enty?* is added for emphasis. In Bajan the almost identical word *ent?* might be added—for example, 'Eunice gone home, ent?'. A similar form of question *You haven't eaten yet, have you?* used to be known in Barbados as 'a Speightstown question'. In spite of the small size of Barbados, regional features and archaisms of speech still exist in certain parts, and Speightstown in the north was always regarded as 'backward' and having certain customs of its own.

Pride and industry,
Bajan 'born and bred'
(*Willie Alleyne*)

Pronunciation

Perhaps the most striking similarity of all is the rendering of words like 'car', 'character' and 'garden' as *kyar*, *kyarakter* and *gyardin*. The word *ask* is rendered *ax* in both places. Clipping of consonants is also common in both, e.g. *cyan* for 'can't', and *poun* for 'pound'. In both areas the result can be a word combination such as *wuffa* ('what for') or *lewwe* ('let we' or 'let us'). Both dialects put an 'n' in front of the word 'use'. Thus *I ent got no nuse for she*, or, as the fruit sellers say in Barbados, *get your nuseful limes*.

Other peculiarities appear in both dialects, for example mispronunciations with special meanings. *Toreckly* is defined by Frank Collymore in *Barbadian Dialect* as: 'directly', always used in the sense of immediately, or at most, in a very short time, e.g. '"*I'll fix this for you toreckly*", says the carpenter, and means it—at the time.' Compare, from the Glossary for *Maum Chrisl' Chaa' stun—A Gullah Story* by Virginia Geraty: '*Tuhreckly*—directly, soon'. Is this coincidence or further support for a common source of Gullah and Bajan dialect, i.e. seventeenth century Barbadian Creole?

Idiom

Although Bajan creole has retained few African words as such, it has a rich collection of idiomatic expressions, which, according to Richard Allsopp, reflect the influence of a strong African language heritage. Burrowes and Allsopp quote a number: *to like somebody bad* (to like somebody very much), *it will be me and you* (we will have a quarrel), *to set up your face* (to frown), and *to bad talk somebody* (to malign somebody). *Lickmout Lou* (pen-name of a local Barbadian writer meaning 'a popular dispenser of local gossip. One who kisses and tells') writes both a daily newspaper column and a local monthly magazine in dialect. Her work is a rich and ready source of such idioms. Some of these are remarkably similar to Gullah expressions. To *study 'e head* (Gullah: to think deeply) is defined in *Barbadian Dialect* by Frank Collymore as: 'Study—to give thought to, to pay attention to . . . studiation: *too much studiation can set a man mad*.' Similarly, *foreday morning* in *Barbadian Dialect* is a 'description of early dawn', while its equivalent in Gullah is *'Fo dayclean* (before daylight).

Some words have acquired the same unconventional meaning, for example both a Charlestonian and a Bajan might say *There was nothing to eat but the bare rice*, meaning 'there was only rice to eat'. Some compound words (which occur in all creole languages) are common to Gullah and Bajan, for example, *bay-side* and *bay-house*, referring to a house by the sea (at Cattlewash or Bathsheba especially, in Barbados!)

Proverbs

Proverbs are short sayings that express some obvious truth or traditional wisdom, often in a metaphorical way—they may be poetic, rhythmic or alliterative. They may warn or encourage, rebuke or console. They are often ages old, and express the universal truths of every culture, but as time goes by new proverbs may be born to meet the distinctive needs of individual societies.

African cultures are particularly rich in proverbs, but with the dominance of English culture and language in Barbados in the days of slavery, much of the vitality of the African folk lore might have been lost. Yet, although current glossaries of Bajan proverbs reveal a fusion of African and English tradition, the African appears dominant. It seems as if the African thought, the allusion, the metaphor, could live on with a new (English) vocabulary. (There are, of course, many examples of proverbs with a unique and very Barbadian flavour or twist).

A number of West African proverbs thus remain alive in almost identical form in Gullah and Bajan. The Mandingo proverb, *It hard for an empty sack to stand upright* has become *Empty sack can't stand upright alone* in Gullah, and *Empty bag cyan stan up nor full wun cyan bend* in Bajan. *More rain, more rest, more cou-cou, less flesh* in Bajan becomes *Mo rain, mo ress, but fair wedder bin bess* in Gullah. One rhyming proverb:

> *Tit for tat, butter fuh fat*
> *(If you kill me dog I kill you cat)*

appears in almost identical form in both places.

The similarities and the differences in dialects of Afro-American or Caribbean creole English have occupied and will continue to fascinate scholars for a long time.

It comes as no surprise to the Bajan who knows the long history of Barbadian emigration, to Charleston and then to other parts of the Eastern United States, to Suriname and to Jamaica, all in the seventeenth century, and later to Trinidad and Guyana, the rest of the Antilles, and in this century to Panama, Brazil, Curacao and Aruba, London, New York and Toronto, to hear a Bajan accent in any part of the world.

But only to Charleston, perhaps, did Barbados export not just people and names, but parish names and street names, the system of local government, crops, a house style, life style and attitudes and the roots of the language. And however much educated Charlestonians may have moved away from the creole, and however decreolised Barbadian speech may have become, with its high literacy rate (98%, it is often claimed), there remains enough in common for the eloquent idiom of a Bajan's or a Charlestonian's *I tell yuh* or *don't study yuh head too much* to be instantly understood by the other.

Postscript on Paradise

Barbados and Charleston had much in common in the seventeenth and early eighteenth centuries: housing, language, life-style, the plantation economy built around slavery and sugar; and not least, a bold, chauvinist pride. Charleston, it has been said '*is* the South ... the Mother City'. And as our story shows, Barbados was in turn the 'Mother of Charleston'.

Charleston grew out of necessity. Overcrowding in Barbados, when there was no more land to be had, led to Captain William Hilton's exploration of the Carolina coast and eventually to the new colony. But to make the settlement work it had to be promoted, and Hilton himself wrote: 'the land we suppose is healthful; for the English that were cast away on that Coast in July last ... notwithstanding hard usage, and lying on the ground naked, yet had their perfect healths all the time.' (Visions of bikini-clad bathers on the beaches of Barbados.)

Others were even more glowing in their praise—William Sayle, the first Governor, wrote to the Proprietors that 'I have been in several places, yet never was in a sweater climate than this is.' Unfortunately, it was not long before the importation of malaria altered the facts and the perception. In the early years over eighty per cent of the population died by the age of twenty and few lived to sixty.

Today of course Charleston is not just healthy but thriving, in a unique and splendid way. Like Barbados it has survived hurricanes, fires and pestilence; even a devastating earthquake (1886) and the Civil War. Its ruin was in fact its saving grace, and by 1920 it had the first Preservation Society in the United States. Charleston's restoration is a shining epic. It succeeded because 'something was sacred about the city'. Notably the city seal reads: 'She guards her buildings, customs and laws'.

Charleston is not just a place of pilgrimage for the rest of the country to see hundreds of historic buildings. It is a 'living growing city'—a model city of adaptive restoration, and the sense of history is real and exciting. In 1986 it was voted 'most livable city in the USA'.

Barbados too is a place of pilgrimage, but more for sun-worshippers than for historical buffs. It too has been extolled as a kind of Paradise. Aspinall's *Pocket Guide to the West Indies* (1907) said 'Barbados is the healthiest of all the West Indian Islands ...' A later traveller and author, Raymond Savage, wrote of it in 1936 'I have discovered the nearest place to perfection that I am ever likely to find in this sad world.'

With its perfect climate (70–85°F year round), stable government, beautiful beaches, landscape and architectural heritage, is it not the most livable country in the world? Indeed the historian Froude, a visitor in 1887, wrote of Bajans: 'They cling to their home with innocent vanity, as though it was the finest country in the world.' Sir Frederick Treves in *Cradle of the Deep*, commented: 'If they do leave it, it is only for a time.'

Barbados was for many years the gateway to America and until the American War of Independence it was literally the main post office for the Carolinas. After colonising Carolina in the seventeenth century many Barbadians have gone further north in later years and New York now has a huge Barbadian community. But today's travellers are chiefly heading in the opposite direction.

The tourist trek south goes back a long way. George Washington brought his brother Lawrence, ill with tuberculosis, here for his health in 1751. Nearly four hundred thousand visitors now come each year for a brief visit (some for their health) and Bajans will wax eloquent explaining why it is 'Paradise on Earth'.

But Barbados is not just sun, sand and sea. Its rich heritage, its natural beauty and its historic buildings and sites comprise a small but, like Charleston, unique place. Unlike Charleston, its architectural heritage is under serious threat as the Philistines, with a limited view of progress, needlessly destroy that heritage. Only a new, enlightened vision can save it.

We hope this little book will help; and that it may strengthen the historical and cultural ties between Barbados and Carolina and bring some of our exciting history to a wider audience.

Bibliography

Chapters 1–7

Alleyne, Warren *Caribbean Pirates* Macmillan Caribbean, London and Basingstoke, 1986

Baldwin, Agnes L. *First Settlers of South Carolina* Southern Historical Press Inc., Easley, S.C., 1985

Bargar, B.D., F.R. Hist. S. *Royal South Carolina, 1719–1763* University of South Carolina Press, Columbia, S.C., 1970

Calendar of State Papers, Colonial Series: *America and the West Indies* Vol. V (1661–1668); Vol. VII (1669–1674) edited by W.N. Sainsbury 1880–1889, Public Record Office, London

Chandler, Alfred D. 'The Expansion of Barbados', *Journal of the Barbados Museum and Historical Society*, Vol. XIII, Nos. 3 & 4, 1946

Cheves, Langdon 'Middleton of South Carolina: a Middleton Family Genealogy', *The South Carolina Historical and Genealogical Magazine*, 1, 227–262, 1900

Cheves, Langdon, editor, *The Shaftesbury Papers and Other Records relating to Carolina and the First Settlement on Ashley River prior to the year 1676* South Carolina Historical Society, Collections, Vol. V, 1987

Defoe, Daniel *A General History of the Pirates* edited by Manuel Schonhorn, originally published in 1724, reprinted by Messrs J.M. Dent & Sons Ltd, London, 1972

Dunn, Richard S. *Sugar and Slaves: The Rise of the planter class in the English West Indies 1624–1713* Jonathan Cape, London, 1973

Dunn, Richard S. 'The English Sugar Islands and the founding of South Carolina', *The South Carolina Historical Magazine* July 1971, Vol. 72, No. 3, pp 81–93

Harlow, Vincent T. *A History of Barbados, 1625–1685* The Clarendon Press, Oxford, 1926

Helwig, Adelaide B. *The Early History of Barbados and her Influence upon the*

Development of South Carolina (Ph.D. diss., University of California, Berkeley, 1931

Hotten, John Camden, editor, *Original Lists of Persons of Quality, 1600–1700* Genealogical Publishing Company Inc., Baltimore, 1980

Hoyos, F.A. *Barbados: a History from the Amerindians to Independence* Macmillan Caribbean, London and Basingstoke 1978

Jones, Lewis P. *South Carolina: A Synoptic History for Laymen* Sandlapper Publishing Inc, Orangeburg, S.C., 1971

Joyner, Charles *Down by the Riverside: A South Carolina Slave Community* University of Illinois Press, Urbana and Chicago, 1984

Lumsden, May *The Barbados-American Connection* Macmillan Caribbean, London and Basingstoke 1988

Middleton Place, Middleton Place National Historic Landmark Inc., 1976

Read, M. Alston 'Notes on some Colonial Governors of South Carolina and their Families', *The South Carolina Historical and Genealogical Magazine*, Vol. XI, No. 1, January 1910, South Carolina Historical Society, Charleston, S.C.

Ripley, Warren *Charles Towne: Birth of a City*, Evening Post Publishing Company, Charleston, S.C., 1970

Rogers, George C. Jr *A South Carolina Chronology, 1497–1970*, University of South Carolina Press, Columbia, S.C., 1973

Rogers, George C. Jr *Charleston in the Age of the Pinckneys* University of South Carolina Press, Columbia, S.C., 1980

Rosen, Robert *A short history of Charleston* Lexikos, San Francisco, 1982

Sirmans, M. Eugene *Colonial South Carolina: A political history, 1663–1763* University of North Carolina Press, Chapel Hill, 1966

South Carolina Genealogies: Vol. II (Colleton – Izard) The Reprint Company, Publishers, Spartanburg, S.C., 1983

Thomas, John P. Jr 'The Barbadians in early South Carolina' *South Carolina Historical Magazine*, Vol. 31, No. 2, April 1930; pp. 75–92

Waring, Joseph I, M.D. *The First Voyage and Settlement at Charles Town, 1670–1680* University of South Carolina Press, Columbia, S.C., 1970

UNPUBLISHED DOCUMENTS

Minutes of (Barbados) Council 20 January 1740/41; 17 February 1740/41; 28 April 1767; 26 January 1769; 18 June 1771; 9 July 1771; 23 August 1771.

Chapter 8 Sir John Yeamans and St Nicholas Abbey

Campbell, Peter F. Editor's Note, *Chapters in Barbados History* The Barbados Museum and Historical Society, Barbados, 54–60, 1986

Fraser, Henry and Hughes, Ronnie *Historic Houses of Barbados* The Barbados National Trust and Art Heritage Publications, Barbados, Second Edition, 1986

Shilstone, Eustace M. 'Nicholas Plantation and some of its associations' in *Chapters in Barbados History*, ed. Peter Campbell, The Barbados Museum and Historical Society, Barbados, 1986

Chapter 9 The Drayton Connection

Hastie, John Drayton *The Story of Magnolia Plantation and its Gardens* Magnolia Plantation, Charleston, 1984

Page, Marian *Historic Houses restored and preserved* Whitney Library of Design, New York, 1981

Chapter 10 The Charleston Single House and the Barbadian Connection

Fraser, Henry S. and Hughes, Ronnie *Historic Houses of Barbados* (2nd Edition) Barbados National Trust and Art Heritage Publications, Barbados, 1986

Gosner, Pamela *Caribbean Georgian* Three Continents Press, New York, 1982

Ligon, Richard *A True and Exact History of the Island of Barbados* (1657) Frank Cass, London, Facsimilie Edition, pp 102–104, 1970

Severens, Kenneth, in *Southern Architecture* ed. R.P. Dulton, New York, 1981

Slesin, Susanne et al *Caribbean Style.* Thames and Hudson, London, 1985

Stoney, Samuel G. (1944), *This is Charleston* Carolina Art Association, Charleston, (Revised Edition) 1976

Chapter 11 Gullah and Bajan Dialect

Alleyne, Mervyn C. *Comparative Afro-American* Karoma Publishers Inc., Ann Arbor, 1980

Blackman, Margot *Bajan Proverbs* Margot Blackman, Montreal, 1982

Burrowes, Audrey, (in collaboration with R. Allsopp), in *Studies in Caribbean Language, Barbadian Creole: its social history and structure* Society for Caribbean Linguistics, c/o School of Education, UWI, St Augustine, Trinidad, 1983

Cassidy, Frederic, in 'The Place of Gullah', *American Speech* 55, 3–16, 1980

Cassidy, Frederic, in 'Sources of the African Element in Gullah' *Studies in Caribbean Language* 1983

Collymore, Frank A. *Barbadian Dialect* (1955) The Barbadian National Trust, (Fifth Edition), 1976

Forde, G. Addington, *De mortar-pestle* The National Cultural Foundation, Barbados, 1987

Hancock, Ian F, in 'Gullah and Barbadian—origins and relationships' *American Speech* 55, 17–35, 1980

Joyner, Charles *Down by the Riverside* University of Illinois Press, Urbana and Chicago, 1984

Lynch, Louis *The Barbados Book* Andre Deutsch, 1964

Index